the Island Kitchen

appetising recipes
from the Isle *of* Man's
finest chefs and
restaurants

EDITORS

Nicola Cowsill attended King William's College on the Isle of Man before reading politics at Northumbria University. Her interests include politics, English, travelling and cycling. She now lives Scotland working for Universities Scotland as a Committee & Policy Assistant.

Sara Donaldson attended the Robert Gordon University in Aberdeen. Following a life as a university librarian in her native North Yorkshire, she returned north and now enjoys life as an editor in the far north of Scotland. Her interests include art, history and cooking… when not working she can usually be found in her local community theatre.

MANAGING EDITOR: **Miles Cowsill**
ART DIRECTOR: **Ian Smith**
PHOTOGRAPHY: **Simon Park, Peter Cubbon and Dept of Environment, Food and Agriculture.**
ACKNOWLEDGEMENTS: **Suzanne Cubbon-Curphey, Richard Slee and Audrey Fowler.**

Lily Publications

Produced in the Isle of Man
by Lily Publications Ltd
Tel: +44 (0) 1624 898446
www.lilypublications.co.uk.

THE ISLAND KITCHEN

The Isle of Man has a rapidly growing international reputation for its outstanding food and drink. Traditionally known for its excellent kippers, the Island also boasts some of the finest seafood anywhere, including its queenie scallops. With the Island being free from intensive farming methods, the quality of the produce is second to none – Loaghtan sheep provide lamb of the highest quality, while the distinctive taste of the Island's milk and cream is reflected in its award-winning dairy products.

The Island Kitchen illustrates the high standard of cuisine that can be found on the Island, showcasing signature dishes from the Isle of Man's finest chefs and restaurants using the abundant, high-quality produce that the Island is renowned for. From succulent starters to delicious desserts, you are sure to find a favourite and keep coming back for more.

CONTENTS

CONTENTS

FOREWORD COLIN CLAGUE

I was born on the Isle of Man, spent my childhood in a rural community and saw for myself the passion that goes into producing the distinctive array of food and drink that is part of our culture.

My mother was a very capable cook and used these commodities on a daily basis to create delicious dishes.

As I forged a career in food, my background inspired me to produce unique and outstanding menus using the best local produce.

I am proud to be Manx, for many reasons.

The Isle of Man is a unique location. It retains the landscape I enjoyed in my childhood and, unlike much of Europe, has not been subject to fertilisers and intensive farming methods.

Our Loaghtan sheep provide some of the highest quality lamb found anywhere. Our fertile fields mean our milk and cream boasts a distinctive taste that is reflected in the success of our dairy exports.

The kipper, for which the Island is traditionally known, is still a favourite for breakfast or making pâté. But around our shores we have a rich diversity of fishing, including our renowned king and queen scallops, which appear on the menus of top restaurants. Our seafood, including crab, lobster and whelk, are enjoyed the world over.

Alongside the traditional food that has underpinned our rural landscape for generations, new entrepreneurs are using local ingredients to create new products.

The Island is developing a great reputation internationally for its outstanding food and drink, the momentum driven by Food Matters, the Isle of Man government's strategy to grow the value of the sector by £50 million.

This book describes how our leading local restaurants are using the quality and diversity of local produce to its best advantage.

It showcases their signature dishes featuring Manx produce, something I have been passionate about since my early days as a chef on the Isle of Man.

I hope you will enjoy this exciting book. The recipes are varied, imaginative and delicious – whether you enjoy them at home or eating out, where they will be lovingly created by our skilled chefs.

Colin Clague
October 2015

CHAPTER 1

INTRODUCTION TO FARMING AND FISHING

When it comes to food, the Isle of Man, like many other parts of Great Britain over the last 20 years, has been increasingly discovering the riches on its own doorstep.

The recipe for any local food culture always has certain basic ingredients – climate, history, economics – and to those the spice is added, that little piquant twist that makes it unique, wherever it happens to be. In the Isle of Man's case, its status as a small island nation and that stretch of water surrounding it are the elements that have brought its own distinctive flavour.

The story of how our Manx food culture, and its unique ingredients, developed really begins in the early days of the 19th century. The Isle of Man, at that time, was not a wealthy place and many Manx people emigrated to America in search of opportunity. For those who stayed, the primary way to make a living and feed their families was through farming and fishing: on the Isle of Man you are never far from the sea and many families would do both.

For the average Manx person in those days food choice would be governed by availability and the need to fill hungry stomachs, but we now know that the ingredients they had access to had a lot to recommend them. Potatoes, grown essentially organically, and herring, from the clear waters around the Island, meant that the local subsistence diet was probably a good deal healthier than that of similarly impoverished people in other parts of the British Isles.

All this changed as the Victorian era ushered in the beginnings of the tourist boom and the Isle of Man was transformed into 'The Holiday Isle', one of the most popular destinations in the British Isles. At its height, in the early 1900s and just after the Second World War, nearly 700,000 people came to visit the Island each year. Black and white newsreels from those heady days show the promenade in Douglas engulfed by crowds. The local population alone could not cope with these numbers and seasonal workers, such as switchboard operators for the telephone exchange, would also be brought in.

All these visitors and workers brought with them not only prosperity for many Manx people but also new ideas about food – things like chips, pies and, of course, 'the full English breakfast'. When local people not only catered to these tastes but adopted them for themselves, it signalled the end of the isolation of their food culture.

Then came the 1960s, when package holidays made travel to Europe affordable and, instead of coming to the Isle of Man, holidaymakers headed off to the Costas for sun and sangria. This coincided with a decline in the fishing industry, the Island's other main employer, and things looked bleak until the Isle of Man reinvented itself as a low tax jurisdiction. This brought real prosperity to the Island: property prices rose and local people saw a huge increase in job opportunities and wages. Where young people going off to university had previously waved goodbye to the Island forever, now they were returning to well paid jobs in the finance sector.

From then on, people on the Isle of Man

broadly followed the same foodie trends as their neighbours, where migration and travel, and the increase in trade around the world, meant that chefs and consumers often looked to places far afield for their ingredients and their flavours.

And they expected to be able to get their hands on every type of fresh produce, whatever the season.

Green beans in the winter? No problem – they could be flown in from Kenya.

Asparagus from Peru; Kiwi fruit from Chile – the list goes on.

But, with the start of the new millennium, something began to change. The phrase 'food miles' entered the vocabulary and the idea of transporting fresh produce halfway across the world began to be seen as something rather less desirable. Chefs and foodies began looking closer to home for their recipe inspiration and with that came a growing awareness of what might be available closer to home.

The Isle of Man began to wake up to the fact that its locally produced food had a lot to offer.

It is, of course, not the only Island in the British Isles that can proudly boast its own 'heirloom' foods. Jersey for example, has delicious new potatoes and rich milk from its indigenous cows.

But just to put it into context: the Isle of Man is nearly 5 times the size of Jersey, with a smaller population. At 572 square km (221 square miles), the Isle of Man is also larger than the Isle of Wight and nearly 10 times the size of Guernsey.

The Isle of Man has the wide open space that Jersey and the other Channel Islands lack and a great deal of that space is occupied, in one form or another, by agriculture. And, despite being further north, its comparatively frost-free climate not only allows palm trees to flourish (the Isle of Man has its own indigenous palm tree) but also helps the local growers and gives rich pastures for its livestock. About 85 per cent of the Isle of Man is given over to agricultural production, with about 450 farms, and you will see the signs of this everywhere as you drive around.

Whether it is sheep grazing on the purple heather hillsides, cows chewing the cud in lush green pastures, or free-range hens clucking by the side of narrow lanes, this is an Island with a big investment, both emotionally and financially, in farming, growing and producing.

Local people love to get out and around the Island, walking and cycling the footpaths and greenways. They see the farming and growing process at first hand and feel close to it and they appreciate that farmers are the guardians of our rich and varied landscape. Consequently, many Islanders feel protective towards the farming industry.

In March 2013, the Island's worst recorded snowfall in 50 years left sheep stranded in drifts 10 feet deep. The word went out on social media that help was needed and a small army of 'snow heroes' responded. The emergency services were joined by hundreds of volunteer helpers who left their office jobs and took up shovels and spades to help.

Even the Island's iconic TT motorcycle races, still a huge visitor draw for two weeks every year, have had to take second place to the interests of maintaining a healthy farming industry. In 2001, when foot-and-mouth disease devastated farms all around Britain, the Island used its geographic isolation to great effect, among other measures cancelling that year's races, and thankfully the Island remained free of the disease.

The inherent loyalty of the Manx public to locally grown and produced products, and the growing acknowledgement of their quality, now has the backing of official government strategy. 'Food Matters' represents the formalising of support for the Island's increasingly entrepreneurial farmers, fishermen, growers, producers and others in the local food and drink industry. It is a recognition of the value of the food industry in the local economy and its potential for growth.

When the strategy was launched, in 2014, Minister for the Environment, Food and Agriculture Richard Ronan MHK said:

Consumers are becoming increasingly sophisticated in their choice of food and drink, for health, economic and environmental reasons, and this can give us a competitive advantage into the future.

Supporting local businesses, taste and quality, knowing where their food has come from – the so-called journey from farm to fork – and food miles and packaging are important to them.

So, let us take a closer look at the Manx food

culture of today, at some of the great food that is produced on the Island and hear the stories behind the labels you will see in local shops and supermarkets and the ingredients listed proudly on restaurant menus.

Make Sure It's Manx Meat

Because the vast majority of livestock is slaughtered on the Island, rather than being shipped to meat plants in the UK, Manx meat is a totally traceable product. From January 2011, an EU ruling meant that the Isle of Man could no longer regulate imports of meat, so consumers now need to ask whether their meat is Manx, instead of taking it for granted. But horrors such as horsemeat in the food chain have given shoppers a greater appreciation of high levels of traceability in what they buy.

Isle of Man Meats runs the Island's meat plant and its Chief Executive, Mike Owen, is a master butcher who has worked in meat plants all over the world before coming to the Island.

He says:

What has struck me coming here is that people on the Island are very passionate about the local farming industry. They're proud of being Manx and they want to buy Manx meat – you wouldn't get that in the UK.

I have no problem with competition from imported meat – if you have to be competitive it makes you do things better. It's actually in our favour because what we do produce is a very high-quality product and there's nothing finer than to know that you're buying meat that's got very low food miles and the animals are not stressed by travelling for long distances. You can also have peace of mind that you're supporting the farming community in the very place that you live, where the meat that you eat has been reared on the very ground that you walk on. Now, who else can say that?

Butchers around the Island already display signs in their shops telling customers which farm the beef, or the lamb, has come from that week and the Island's own supermarket chain, Shoprite, a great supporter of local meat and produce, sells Manx-reared and produced meat under its Ballacushag Farms label.

Isle of Man Meats wants to make this traceability even more transparent to consumers. It is introducing a logo to go on all packaged meat which clearly indicates that it has been reared and produced on the Island. The plan is to back this up with an auditing system, which will mean that each pack also has a number that consumers can type into Isle of Man Meats' website and see for themselves exactly which farm it has come from. Taking the idea a stage further, this will also help restaurants to link this traceability to their menus, so that the steak on the specials board that evening might also have the name of the farm it came from beside it.

Another characteristic that chefs are looking for more and more in their meat is a marbling of fat, which gives extra flavour, and this tends to be found more in the traditional British breeds of cattle.

John and Alison Teare, who farm at Ballavair, in Bride, took the decision to convert their cattle from continental breeds to the Black Galloway, a native breed more usually found in the highlands of Scotland. Ballavair is on the north coast of the Island, with sandy and free-draining soil, but the Galloways have thrived there, their double coat allowing them to cope quite happily with the wind blowing in off the sea.

Time is the key factor in rearing traditional beef cattle the way nature intended, explains Alison Teare:

Because of it being a native breed, we're trying to recreate how beef used to be. So it was really important that we also had a traditional butcher involved (W E Teare's in Ramsey) who understood the process of hanging and ageing. When you've taken so long making sure it gets to the right stage, that end process is just as important.

It's slow-grown and slow-maturing so, although it is no more expensive than other Manx beef, it will never be a mass-market product: it's something that's available only when it's ready and at its best.

At its best it is very good indeed: in 2014, Ballavair Galloway received a two-star Gold Award for their rolled rib of beef at the Great Taste Awards, the British Isles' most prestigious food awards scheme. Alison says: 'We're very, very lucky on the Island: all the meat produced here is fantastic – ours is just something a little bit different.'

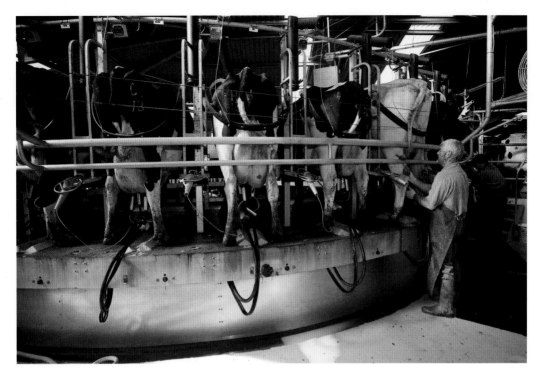

If you love a good banger, or a slice of traditionally-cured bacon, you can find traceability in these products, too, on the Island. Alan Teare farms around 420 acres at Ballakelly, in Andreas, where he lives with his partner Rachel and their two young children. Alan took over from his father, Billy, who is now retired, and is the fourth generation of his family to run the farm. Alan has around 100 breeding sows: his barn-raised piglets grow at an astonishing rate and reach their required weight of 75–80kg in just a few short months.

All his pork goes to the Andreas Meat Company, just along the road from the farm, where it is used for bacon, a variety of sausages and cooked, sliced gammon. They are all delicious and reflect the care that has been taken, both in the rearing of the animals and in the making of the final product. 'With sausages you only get out what you put in. It's a meticulous process and we weigh everything to the ounce. That care is what makes it a completely consistent product', says Norman Morrey, owner of Andreas Meat Company.

Norman knows pork and sausages inside out: he started a pig farm on the Island in 1953 and has been making sausages for the last 10 years.

His sausage recipe is 90 years old and uses around 70 per cent meat, which experience has shown him to be the ideal. He adds: 'Our sausages don't shrink when you cook them – they come out of the pan the same size as they went in. So does our bacon because it's all dry-cured.'

Much of the landscape on the Isle of Man is ideally suited to the raising of sheep, and Manx lamb has been always been popular on the Island. Will and Janette Qualtrough, owners of the Ballakarran Meat Company, manage a flock of more than 500 pedigree Charolais and cross black face ewes and sell boxed lamb direct from the farm. Their sheep are pasture-fed and Will believes the Isle of Man is ideally suited to this very natural way of rearing and producing lamb. He says:

Because we sit in the Gulf Stream and we also have quite high rainfall, our climate lends itself to growing grass very well, sometimes for 11 or even 12 months of the year. In addition, a lot of the land we farm is coastal land and the winds blowing in off the sea lace the grass with salt spray, which is full of trace elements and minerals so it's the perfect environment for producing really tasty lamb.

The Island's own indigenous sheep breed, the Loaghtan, distinguishable by its 'mouse brown' coat (after which it is named) and spectacular horns, also produces good meat.

Sam Quilleash raises Loaghtans on his parents' farm in Ballaragh, high above Laxey bay, a gorse-scented landscape looking east over the sea towards Cumbria. The Quilleash family have been farming this land since records began on the Isle of Man in the 1400s. Sam says: 'All our Loaghtans are pasture-fed with no substitute feeding to fatten them up and they all drink from a spring which has always been on our land. We don't use pesticides and only minimal fertilisers.'

Unlike commercial sheep breeds, which are killed in their first year, Loaghtans will not reach a suitable size until they are between 18 months and 3 years old. This slow growing contributes to the rich flavour, for which it is valued along with the lack of fat. Loaghtan meat is delicious roasted and in casseroles and it makes great burgers.

It's not just the traditional and indigenous livestock which thrive on the Isle of Man. Clare Lewis and her partner Mike Walker run a herd of 250 South African Boer goats in Kirk Michael. Boer goats are the world's premier breed for goat meat and their herd is one of the largest in the British Isles. All the meat they sell comes from goats born and raised on their farm where they are predominantly grass-fed. Goats are surprisingly tricky to rear, always needing shelter from the rain, for example, and the emphasis is very much on welfare. Goat meat, which is becoming increasingly popular, has less saturated fat than skinless chicken and is also high in protein and iron, as well as being very tasty.

Gourmet Riches from the Sea

Historically, the fish of choice for Manx people – and one of their diet staples – was the herring. The reason for this was simple: these fish ran in shoals and so were easy to catch in great numbers. In the days before refrigeration, these oily fish, unlike fresh white fish, could be salted down and stored through the winter. Then, in the 1830s, another method of preserving was discovered – smoking – and the Manx kipper was born.

Paul Desmond owns Moore's Kippers, the only remaining traditional kipper factory on the Island. Here, they source only the optimum type of herring – those with a 16 ½ – 17 ½ per cent oil content – and, once they reach Manx shores, Moore's Kippers hang them over oak fires just as they would have done in those early days. 'My yard was built in 1882', says Paul. 'The traditional methods we use take a lot longer but Moore's is renowned for having the best kippers. We're trying to do small quantities of the best.'

Nowadays the Isle of Man is known around the world for a rather more sophisticated item of riches from its seas – the queen scallop, or queenie. This tiny delicacy has become massively popular, both on the Island and in restaurants around Europe. Each year, the Isle of Man exports around £8m worth of queenies and the industry currently supports around 150 jobs at sea and 200 on land. The Manx queenie has been awarded Protected Designation Origin (PDO) status by the EU, much like products such as Gorgonzola cheese and Champagne.

The Isle of Man, backed by specific scientific research, was an early adopter of sustainable fishing practices.

'The Isle of Man fishing industry started its conservation practices many years ago in the late 1970s', says William Caley, manager of Isle of Man Seafoods, 'The UK only has one per cent of its waters under protection, whereas nearly half of Manx waters have protection measures.'

Isle of Man Seafoods has a fleet of seven boats fishing for queenies. Like all the Manx fishing fleets they fish only with nets, rather than dredge gear which damages the sea bed by bringing everything along in its wake. This means that they can only fish in season, from July to the end of October, when the queenies leave the seabed to feed. Other sustainability measures have included designating closed areas of the Manx coastal waters for queenie fishing and fishing each on an annual rotational basis.

William Caley is one of three generations of his family working together at Isle of Man Seafoods, along with a staff of over 140. They have established a processing plant in Peel for their own boats and other vessels in the Manx fishing fleet, so that queenies caught in season can be frozen within minutes of being landed, thus ensuring a consistent, year-round supply for customers.

There are seemingly innumerable ways of cooking queenies but William says he likes them with chorizo and noodles: 'And they're fine raw' he adds.

Great Veggies – Fewer Food Miles

Wholesalers Robinson's supply Shoprite supermarkets, and also their own retail shops around the Island, with vegetables, fruit and fish. They buy locally wherever possible, from a number of suppliers, including potato grower Les Neil, vegetable grower Stewart Allanson and Mark and Kathy Irwin, owners of Greeba Mushrooms, who produce around 8,000 lbs of mushrooms a week, all for the local market. 'Our mushrooms are picked and ready to go into local shops within hours,' says Kathy, 'when you get them this fresh, they won't go soggy when you cook them.'

Bryan Radcliffe, known to one and all as 'Bry Rad', has been growing vegetables since he left school. He farms 50 acres in Andreas and every Thursday he picks the best of his crop to sell at his Fresh Veg Shed, on the Quay in Ramsey. Bry has built up a big local following on social media with pictures of hedgehogs, farm animals and quirky faces made out of vegetables. On one occasion, when he happened to mention that he had a huge amount of Brussels sprouts to harvest single-handed, he was inundated with offers of help. Bry says:

I started the Facebook page because I wanted to show people the effort that goes into producing veg, because a lot of people get a bit detached from food production. Even though this is only a small island, there's so much that can be produced.

I grow 25 different varieties of vegetables, summer and winter. I grow in the traditional manner, following proper field rotation. My father was a horticulturalist, my grandfather was a farmer, so I do what they taught me to do. You look after the soil with plenty of manure because it gives you a living, then you don't need to use all the chemicals.

I'm very old-fashioned – for me, it's all about people enjoying food.

Bry's average field size is small – just two acres – but with good hedges to provide shelter for the crops and a natural corridor for wildlife. Ladybirds are encouraged because they eat the greenfly. As one fan of his produce wrote on his page: 'These are the ultimate in carefully cultivated courgettes and carrots, perfectly ploughed potatoes and liberally loved leeks. Food miles? Not a problem!'.

Giving Dairy Farmers a Fair Deal

Isle of Man Creamery is the main supplier of home-produced milk and dairy produce on the Island. It's a small co-operative of 31 family-owned dairy farms, the furthest of which is probably not more than 20 miles from the Creamery, so the milk really couldn't be fresher.

It's good for the farmers, too, as they tend to be on higher-paid contracts than some of their counterparts in the British Isles.

The Creamery takes in 22 million litres of milk each year and around 7 million litres are sold on the Island as liquid milk. The remainder goes into cheese, with excess cream being processed into butter or sold as cream.

The big success story has been Isle of Man Creamery's range of cheeses, winners of numerous industry awards. Creamery Chief Executive, Findlay Macleod, explains:

We can trace the history of cheese making on the Isle of Man back to Viking times and our cheese making today reflects those traditional skills. Currently we make about 1,400 tonnes of cheese each year: 300 tonnes are sold on the Island and the rest is exported to the UK, the US, Malta, the Middle East, and Ireland.

Our mature Cheddar is very popular in the US – it's a great, creamy full-flavoured cheese – but they have recently got a bit of a taste for our vintage Cheddar, too.

The provenance is a crucial part of our selling story in terms of the location and the heritage of the Island – it's a great story.

Not all the milk produced on the Island goes to Isle of Man Creamery. Cronk Aalin Farm is situated one mile up a winding unmade lane, nearly 5,000 feet above sea level with glorious views over the Northern plain and across the sea to Ireland. Here, Carl Huxham's dairy cows graze on rich pasture and drink water from a spring. He and his wife, Sarah, have turned some

old cattle sheds into a state-of-the-art dairy where he bottles his milk in traditional one pint bottles with foil tops. It has proved to be a big success and Carl now has four vans delivering Aalin Dairy milk to 500 customers in the north of the Island.

'We have to look to the future,' says Carl, 'we are no longer solely farmers. We are food producers.'

Our Daily Bread

You might not imagine that somewhere as small as the Isle of Man would be producing the wheat for a premium range of flour, popular not only on the Island but also with Michelin-starred chefs in London. But it does.

'Our flour is completely traceable: we have 12 farmers growing for us and I can trace our products to every farm', says Sandra Donnelly, Managing Director of Laxey Glen Mills, 'We export a couple of tons of flour every six weeks to restaurants in London. The chefs value this traceability and also the absence of any additives.'

Regulations governing the production of flour in the UK require that a number of additional ingredients, such as calcium carbonate and iron be added to flour. No such regulations exist on the Island and flour produced at Laxey Glen Mills is a completely pure product.

The Island's largest bakery, Ramsey Bakery, buys 90 per cent of the flour the mill produces. Their bread is sold in supermarkets and convenience stores all over the Island.

The Island's artisan bakery, Noa Bakehouse, also uses Laxey Glen flour and owners Miles and Pippa Pettit are passionate about their products.

Miles used to work in the film industry and, when he gave it up three years ago to come to the Island and bake sourdough bread, it might have seemed a risky change of direction but people on the Island love his loaves and Noa is going from strength to strength. Their signature loaf is the Manx Wild, made with 50 per cent white and 50 per cent wholemeal flour.

Another product that uses Laxey Glen Mills flour is the UK's top-rated Christmas pudding, as made by Karl Berrie in the south of the

Island. Karl took a recipe for Christmas pudding that had been passed down through his mother's family and adapted it using Manx ingredients – butter, eggs, beer, cider and flour – until he decided he had come up with the perfect pud.

Judges at the Great Taste Awards, run by the Guild of Fine Food in the UK, agreed with him, awarding his Christmas pudding with Champagne Cognac their highest accolade – the three-star Gold Award – for three years running. At this year's awards, Berries Christmas puddings and cakes won no fewer than nine awards

Everything in Karl's puddings is made from scratch, right down to the 60–70kg of bread he bakes every day to be crumbed for the puddings: 'When people ask us why we've been the highest-awarded Christmas pudding in the British Isles, it's purely because we don't compromise – we refuse to. Simple as that', says Karl.

Healthy Bees and Clucking Good Eggs

There are more than 80 registered beekeepers on the Island and they are indeed blessed. Not only do their bees have an abundance of gorse, heather, fuchsia and other wildflowers to gather pollen from, they are also free from the dreaded, virus-carrying Varroa mite, which has devastated bee numbers in other parts of the world.

'As an island we have managed to avoid having the Varroa mite here by having a ban on the importation of bees since 1988', explained Pat Shimmin, secretary of the Isle of Man Beekeepers Federation. 'We are the only area of the British Isles to have this ban, which has been ratified by the EU.'

The absence of the Varroa mite also means that beekeepers on the Island, unlike their counterparts in other parts of the UK and Europe, don't have to deal with it through the use of insecticides: 'So our honey is as pure as can be', added Pat.

Egg producers on the Island are also fortunate in that the Island has no foxes. This is the reason why you will often see hens pecking by the roadside in country areas and why good quality free-range eggs are widely available in shops and at farm gates.

Mark Baines and Tracey Gelling farm 37

acres of land in Baldrine. Since 2004, their free-range egg business has grown steadily and they now have between 6,000 and 7,000 hens, all free to roam outdoors. They produce 30,000 eggs a week, all packed on-site. Mark's recipe for good quality eggs is simple: 'Good husbandry, good feed and good pasture', he says.

Quenching Your Thirst

A good pint is one thing you can be sure of on the Isle of Man. And, like so many other Manx food and drink products there is admirable transparency regarding what has gone into your glass of ale.

Rob Storey, owner of microbrewery Hooded Ram, produces a range of craft beers, bottled and on tap. Like other brewers on the Island, his ingredients have to conform to the Isle of Man Pure Beer Act of 1874. Rob explained:

This means that we can't use any substitute for malt, hops, water or sugar. We can only ever use those four basic ingredients. We can't use any flavouring syrups, though the law does allow for the use of certain special added ingredients, like the oysters we used in our Black Pearl Oyster Stout, which won first prize at this year's CAMRA Isle Of Man Beer Festival.

Oysters – really?

'This was an historic idea from the days when oysters were abundant: they add a creaminess to the beer and also a slight hint of sea saltiness', said Rob.

Another of his bottled beers which has become very popular is his Pale Rider Ale, specially formulated for TT fortnight: this is credited with having converted a number of former lager drinkers into real ale enthusiasts.

Around 30 per cent of Hooded Ram beers are sold bottled in stores around the Island. The remainder is available on tap at most of the Island's free houses: look out for Seven Dirty Blondes, another very popular brew, which incorporates seven different varieties of hops.

Will Faulds and Charlotte Traynor run the Apple Orphanage, just outside Peel. They make a range of single-variety apple juices, fruit pressés and real Manx dry cider from fruits they grow themselves or acquire via their fruit exchange. 'If anyone has any excess fruit they can pick it when it's nice and ripe and bring it to us. We will weigh it and then let them choose some of our drinks to take away in exchange', explains Charlotte.

She and Will are always experimenting with different flavours for their drinks and they have recently been trialling two new pressés: Cherry, Manx Elderflower and Cinnamon, and Redcurrant, Manx Elderflower and Rosehips, which are proving very popular.

Manx Food Products Not to Miss

Moore's Kipper Factory and Shop, Peel: kippers, fresh crab meat and crab claws, and traditional smoked bacon.

Manx Honey: many local beekeepers are happy to sell their honey, so the Isle of Man Beekeepers Federation has designed an online Honey Map, showing the locations some of the local producers. www.iombeekeepers.com

Ballakarran Meat Company: pasture-fed, boxed lamb – www.ballakarran.com

Ballaragh Farm Ltd: boxed Loaghtan lamb – 07624 474747

Ballavair Galloway traditional beef: W E Teare Butchers, Parliament Street, Ramsey.

Andreas Meat Company: bacon and a range of sausages, including Cumberland and Manx Dragon – available from Shoprite and convenience stores under their own label and also on Shoprite butchery counters under the Ballacushag Farms label.

Shoprite: a wide range of products from local producers, including Manx-reared and produced meat under their Ballacushag Farms label, Greeba mushrooms, fresh bread from Ramsey Bakery and Noa Bakehouse, and a range of Laxey Glen Mills flour for home baking and bread making.

Isle of Man Creamery: milk, butter, cream and cheeses, including Vintage Cheddar and Black Peppercorn, widely available in local stores, including Shoprite and the Co-op.

*For more information download **Food Matters** from www.gov.im/foodanddrink*

CHAPTER 2

MANX FOOD THEN AND NOW

Ask anybody on the Island what they think of as traditional Manx food and the answer will be, dependent on age, Spuds and Herrin' or Chips, Cheese and Gravy.

Herring has been the staple diet of Manx people for as long as fishermen have been able to fish. The herring fishing traditionally started at the end of May with the season running until October, bringing a bountiful supply of food and plenty of work for Manx families. The vision of hundreds of tiny fishing boats around the coastline in the evenings, with their lights twinkling, was a reassuring sight to behold.

Before the smoking of kippers the traditional Manx dish was always Spuds and Herrin' sometimes known as *Priddhas an Herrin,* but this would often be imaginatively turned into such dishes as herring broth and Fatherless Pie (a

potato and pastry pie).

Most crofters would have kept a cow to feed the family with meat and dairy. Buttermilk was used in many dishes and is still used in the making of the local bread known as bonnag.

Other well-known dishes were binjean, or curds and whey, eaten as a pudding sprinkled with sugar, furmity, a type of porridge, and tanrogans or small scallops.

In the following section you will find the most popular Manx foods that can still be seen on menus today.

Manx Bonnag (Fruit or Plain)

The earliest mention of bonnag in Manx history was in 1629, although it had been around for a good few millennia before then.

It is traditionally a flat-ish, plate-sized unleavened 'loaf', basically consisting of oat-flour or barley-flour mixed with water, 'skim' (whey milk) or buttermilk, depending on what was available, and cooked on a griddle or pot-oven. Sometimes a 'middlin skutch' of lard was also added along with a pinch of salt. The traditional ingredients are Manx flour, lard, carbonate of soda, buttermilk or sour milk and cream of tartar.

Bonnag was the staple diet of the Manx along with a fair broth, herrin' and potato (*praise as keddyn*).

By the 1840s cream of tartar was being added to give it a popular 'bubbly' texture. Also currants or 'French berries' were now widely available, even to the Manx crofter's wife, and thus the classic bonnag was given an 'exotic' upgrade. There is a

continual debate as to whether the addition of dried fruit constitutes a true bonnag, with stalwarts shuddering at the mere mention of a juicy currant or flamboyant sultana.

The hotly contested World Bonnag Baking Championships are still held in Dalby, on the west coast of the Island, in March, every year.

MANX BROTH

> *'I don't know how to make it,*
> *but I know when it's good'*
> *(A H Laughton, former High Bailiff of Peel,*
> *on the topic of Manx Broth, 1905)*

Manx Broth was always the traditional dish served at weddings, often made by the bride herself to prove her prowess at the hearth. It wasn't a proper wedding feast if there was no broth to sup, and could only bode trouble ahead, with much tutting and shaking of bonneted heads, should it be absent.

The broth would be served in 'piggins' (wooden bowls) and supped with 'sligs' (mussel shells).

A fine hearty broth was the cornerstone of Manx daily life consisting of scrag-end of mutton or beef shank, or sometimes both, plus the marrowbone, if such was available, and a goodly measure of barley, carrot, turnip, thyme, leek or celery and parsley, according to a 1908 Manx recipe book. There are various family versions with the addition of secret herbs and suchlike, and there is also talk of ham being added in some quarters.

Manx Loaghtan Lamb

The Loaghtan sheep, is a rare breed multi-horned sheep that is native to the Island. Usually the male rams will have four horns but have been known to have up to six. The name Loaghtan comes from the Manx words, *lugh dhoan*, which mean mouse brown and relates to the colour of the fleece. The meat is unusual in that it is best eaten as mutton. It is lower in fat and cholesterol than most breeds and because of the type of hill grazing it is rich in flavour. Loaghtan lamb has been on sale in Harrods and many top chefs, including the celebrity chefs 'the Hairy Bikers', are known to be particularly fond of cooking with it.

Manx Queenies

Another Manx delicacy are queenies or tanrogans, which are small scallops. They have been awarded the Protected Designation of Origin (PDO) status by the European Commission, which means that scallops landed anywhere other than the Isle of Man cannot be called Isle of Man queenies. Such are their popularity that a Queenie Festival is held every year in the little fishing village of Port St. Mary in the south of the Island.

KIPPER BAP OR KIPPER PÂTÉ

Oh the herrin' boys, the herrin' boys,
the herrin' boys for me,
Red or kippered, fresh or pickled
The herrin's the king of the sea
(Traditional Manx song)

Next to the TT races and Manx cats, the Isle of Man is famous for its kippers. A visitor to the Island will find that their holiday is not complete without a visit to Peel to see kippers being smoked the traditional way.

Kippers have been, and still are, a popular export of the Island, with holiday makers buying them vacuum packed to be posted all over the world.

Kipper pâté is delicious served on a slab of toasted bonnag.

CRAB BAPS

Always a sign of being at the seaside, a favourite pastime for children and adults was searching for crabs in rock pools.

Crabs can be found all around the Island but understandably, due to it being a fishing village, Peel is traditionally the home of the Crab Bap. The crab fishing season runs from April to November, when they are caught by local fisherman using small lobster pots. However, subject to weather conditions, they are usually available throughout the year, with those caught in the seas around the Island considered to be some of the finest in the world.

Unless you are proficient in dressing crab then the meat might be best bought freshly prepared. Mix all the ingredients to a course paste then serve in a locally-made fresh bap, bread roll, sandwich etc. with fresh salad and eat whilst sitting outside taking in the smells of salty Manx sea air. Beware of seagulls who are particularly fond of this hand held food of Manx deliciousness.

CHIPS, CHEESE AND GRAVY

This modern tradition, served in all local fish and chip shops and on offer in numerous cafés, started out as the ideal alternative to kebabs after coming out of the pubs and nightclubs. The original is always served with gravy but curry sauce is also an option. Thought to be a comparatively recent fad, this dish has actually been popular in Canada since the 1950s where it is known as poutine. The name translates as 'hot mess', which is a very apt description. The McDonald's fast food restaurant chain in Canada even has it on its menus. The dish in the Isle of Man has become quite an internet sensation, even having a Facebook page dedicated to it, and anyone who decries the actual thought of trying it will be totally hooked on it if they succumb. Chips, Cheese and Gravy is ideally consumed by sharing with a close friend using two forks and fighting over the best stringy, cheesy bits. It must be made using grated Manx cheese (yes, it really does matter).

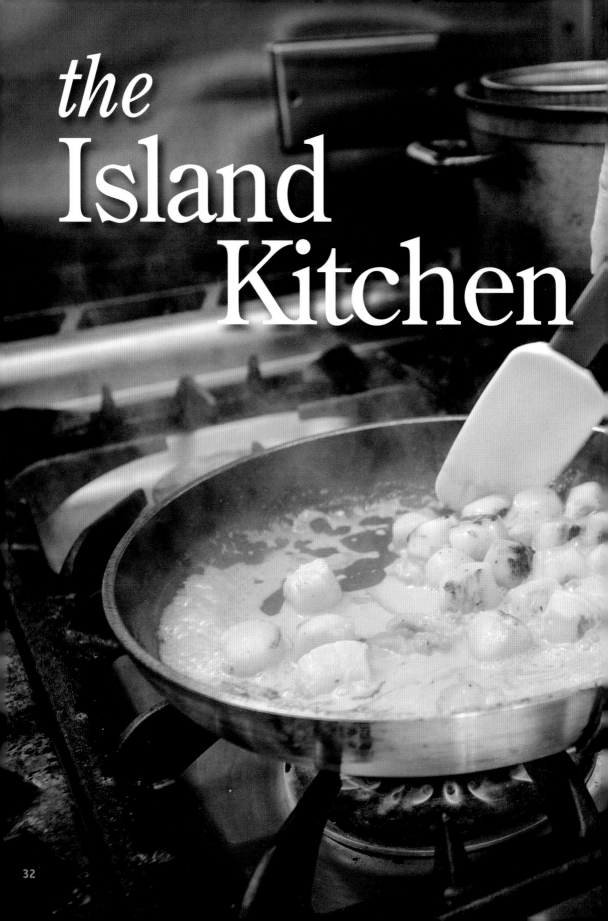

the Island Kitchen

THE COURTHOUSE

Athol Street, Douglas, Isle of Man IM1 1LD
01624 672555
www.the-courthouse.com

The Courthouse restaurant, bar and club is one of the premier venues on the Isle of Man, providing quality food, wines, cocktails and an extensive range of spirits and beers in a contemporary and stylish location.

We are proud to have been awarded the Isle of Man Tourism's 'Taste Isle of Man' award for the highest quality food, interior and service for the last six years, in fact every year since we opened. Our business has also been featured and highly commended in many national newspapers such as *The Times*, *Daily Mail*, *The Guardian*, *Irish Times*, *The Express* and *Metro* magazine and was also chosen as the venue of the month in the *BBC Good Food* magazine and *Olive* magazine.

In our restaurant we have chosen to focus on classic British cuisine with a European influence; all of the dishes on the menu have been specially selected to please. We believe that food should be a pleasure, so we have focused on popular dishes that allow the amazing local produce we have sourced to shine through without us trying to be too clever. We are blessed with some exceptionally good local suppliers, so all of our dishes are made to order using the best and freshest ingredients we can source. Every single dish, including all of our pastries and desserts, is made in-house by our talented chefs, lead superbly by our Head Chef James Stubbs, Isle of Man Chef of the Year for 2015. Even the sauces for the meat dishes are made the old-fashioned way, with stocks and bones reduced to a flavour-packed jus – it is just basic old-school quality cooking created with the best fresh local ingredients.

Our extensive wine list has been provided exclusively for us on the Island by Corney and Barrow, who have expertly matched our wines to complement our dishes and provide a solid and reasonably priced offer. Corney and Barrow have had the Royal Assent for 330 years and provide wines for the royal family, meaning we have access to some belting wines which our local competition cannot match.

Our purpose is simple: to provide amazing food with warm and friendly service, gorgeous drinks and old-fashioned friendly hospitality at a reasonable price in a stunning building. Hopefully, and judging by our reviews and customer feedback, we seem to be achieving this. Come and give us a try and let me know if you agree.

Andy Hardy and the Courthouse team.

The Courthouse

QUEENIES AND PANCETTA WITH SUN BLUSHED TOMATO DRESSING

SERVES 4

Ingredients

Sun Blushed Tomato Dressing
50g good quality sun blushed tomatoes
5g caper berries
1 tsp Dijon mustard
dash white wine vinegar
seasoning to taste

Main Dish
100g pancetta (diced)
400g fresh queenies
60g rocket (washed)
1 tbsp sun blushed tomato dressing (see above)
olive oil for cooking
salt and pepper

Method

For the Dressing
Using a food processor, add the sun blushed tomatoes, caper berries and Dijon mustard. Blend until smooth then add the white wine vinegar and seasoning to taste. This should taste rich, sweet and sharp.

Cooking and Finishing
Heat a frying pan over a high heat with a teaspoon of oil, add the pancetta and lightly brown off before adding the queenies. Remember they don't take long so make sure not to overcook them (one minute should be enough, you will know when they have cooked as they will have a spring to the touch).
Remove the pan from the heat. Using the same pan add the rocket and a tablespoon of the sun blushed dressing then toss together, wilting the rocket ever so slightly. Add seasoning and more olive oil if required.
Plate up and enjoy.

SLOW ROASTED BELLY PORK

SERVES 4

Ingredients

Main Dish
1.2kg (approx.) good quality pork belly
2 white onions
1 bunch of fresh sage
1 bunch of fresh thyme
6 cloves garlic
750ml white wine
500g new potatoes (peeled)
1 bunch of fresh mint
200g fine green beans
knob of butter
parsley (chopped)
salt and pepper

Apple Slaw
5 Cox apples (peeled)
40g caster sugar
1 small white cabbage (grated)
knob of butter
salt and pepper

To Serve
your own family gravy recipe

Method

For the Main Dish
Preheat oven to 200°C/gas 6
First score the fat of the pork using a sharp knife and rub rock salt into the fat. Roughly chop your onions, sage, thyme and garlic and add to a large deep tray, and season. Place the pork belly on top and add the white wine and some water to the tray, making sure you don't pour any liquid over the fat, and leaving the fat above the liquid. Put in the oven for 45 minutes at 200°C, then lower the temperature to 140–150°C for an additional 2 hours 15 minutes. Make sure to keep topping the tray up with water throughout this time.

For the Apple Slaw
Whilst the pork is in the oven, start with the apple slaw. Roughly chop the apples into 2cm chunks, add to a saucepan with 20ml of water and the caster sugar and cook for approx. 20 minutes until the apples become soft. In another saucepan lightly sauté the grated cabbage in a little butter for 2–3 minutes, making sure the cabbage keeps its crunch. When the apples are cooked mash together to form an apple sauce and combine with the cabbage. Reheat later when putting the dish together.

To Finish
After the 2 hours 15 minutes cooking time, turn the oven temperature back up to 200°C and allow the fat to crisp up for a further 20–30 minutes. Boil your new potatoes in seasoned water, adding the mint, for approx. 20 minutes, and simmer the fine beans for 4 minutes. Drain the potatoes when cooked and roughly crush with a little butter, chopped parsley and seasoning.
Finally remove the pork belly into generous portions, plate up with the potatoes and beans, and serve with a jug of lovely homemade gravy.

ASSIETTE OF CHOCOLATE: FONDANT, MOUSSE & TRUFFLE

SERVES 4

Ingredients

Fondant (makes 4)
55g dark chocolate (80% cocoa solids) (broken into small pieces)
65ml whipping cream
30g caster sugar
1 egg
2 egg yolks
4 two-inch buttered and cocoa-lined ramekins

Sesame Snap Topped Chocolate Mousse
Sesame Snap (makes 10)
225g caster sugar
4 tbsp water
100g sesame seeds
non-stick tray (oiled)

Chocolate Mousse (makes 8)
70g butter (cut into pieces)
225g dark chocolate (80% cocoa solids) (broken into small pieces)
350ml double cream
2 large eggs
2 tbsp good honey
1 tbsp Amaretto
8 shot glasses

Chocolate Truffle (makes 25)
200ml whipping cream
175g dark chocolate (70% cocoa solids) (broken into small pieces)
50g unsalted butter
cocktail sticks (optional but it will get messy without them)
a little cocoa powder for rolling

Truffle Coating
200g dark chocolate (80% cocoa solids) (melted over a pan of warm water)

Method

For the Fondant
Preheat oven to 160°C°/gas 3
Place your buttered ramekins in a tray.
Put the chocolate pieces into a glass bowl with the cream. Heat a pan with a small amount of water and place the bowl on top, being careful not to let the water touch the bowl. Carefully melt together.
Follow the same steps for the sugar, egg and yolks but this time whisk with an electric whisk. Remove from the heat and continue whisking until light and fluffy. This may take 8–10 minutes.
Very carefully fold ⅓ of the egg mix into the chocolate. Fold in the last ⅔ to make a silky, fluffy chocolate mixture.
Pour your mixture into each ramekin until it is ¾ full. This will allow for the raise. Bake for 5–6 minutes. They are ready when a crust has been formed but still have a wobble when moved.
Dust with cocoa powder and arrange on your plate.

Sesame Snap Topped Chocolate Mousse
For the Sesame Snap
Warm the sugar and water over a medium heat in a saucepan. They will quickly become a syrup and this should be cooked until lightly browned. Add the sesame seeds and carry on cooking until rich golden brown.
Spread the mix out 0.5cm deep onto the oiled tray. Cool for 15 minutes in the fridge and then break up into shards suitable for topping the mousse.

For the Chocolate Mousse
Melt the butter and chocolate in a heatproof bowl over a pan of warm water. In a separate bowl whisk the cream until a soft peak is formed. In a third bowl whisk the eggs and honey.
Add the Amaretto to the egg mixture then add half the cream and fold gently. Add all the ingredients to the largest bowl and fold gently so as not to knock too

much air out. Once the whole mix is a lovely chocolate brown, pour into the shot glasses.

For the Chocolate Truffle

Carefully bring your cream to the boil and then add the chocolate and butter, stirring continuously until completely smooth.

Allow the mix to cool for 20 minutes before covering and leaving in the fridge for 2 hours to set completely. Remove from the fridge and spoon good teaspoon-sized pieces onto a greaseproof-lined tray. Place the tray back into the fridge to reset the truffle mixture. After the small pieces have set firm, dust them and your hands with a little cocoa powder. They will melt quickly in your hands so it is best to work quite fast (though the tray can go in and out of the fridge as you work).

Roll the pieces into neat balls, re-dusting your hands as you go.

Put the tray of rolled truffles into the fridge to reset before coating. While they are setting, put a cocktail stick about halfway into each. Line a second tray with greaseproof paper while you are waiting for them to firm up.

Take your bowl of melted chocolate and carefully place one truffle at a time into the chocolate by holding the cocktail stick. Remove straight away, wait for the drips to stop, then place onto the grease-proofed tray. Once you have finished cool for one last time.

To Serve

We arrange this dessert on a large plate in either a line or in a triangle. It really doesn't need much garnish as each part speaks for itself.

14 NORTH

14 North Quay, Douglas, Isle of Man IM1 4LE
01624 664414
www.14north.im

14 North, part of the Rock Food Concepts group, opened its doors in August 2010 with the simple aim of showcasing the finest produce the Isle of Man's farmers and artisanal suppliers have to offer. Though a few things have changed since we first launched five years ago, our commitment to seasonal, fresh and locally sourced produce remains our biggest driving force – for everyone, from our kitchen team through to our head chef and our friendly and welcoming front of house staff.

We are located on Douglas' North Quay in a beautiful old Manx building that has been redesigned using zinc, wood and brick to provide a laid back setting for any event; whether an express business lunch, candlelit date night or a celebratory meal with friends. We always strive to provide the warmest possible welcome and genuine hospitality, no matter what the occasion.

We believe in keeping things simple and honest; yet delicious. The food scene on the Island has continued to go from strength to strength and we have a bigger selection than ever of local food and drink options, new eateries and passionate producers.

Delicious food is at the heart of everything we do at 14North. It's the reason we joined the hospitality world and it's our passion first and foremost.

We use the freshest possible produce and treat all of our produce with respect; using simple cooking methods in order to let the produce be the star of any dish.

We don't have a specific type of cuisine so the style of food we serve is best described as 'Modern British'; great seasonal flavours that take inspiration from our melting pot culture. The Island is brimming with quality seafood and great meat such as the Loaghtan lamb we have showcased on our menus since our opening day. Vegetables are delivered through our front door every Thursday from 'up North' and Bryan Radcliffe is always happy to chat to our customers about his crop.

Gaining international recognition in recent years is the Island's largest export – queen scallops or 'queenies'. These beautiful little sweet, tender scallops are a staple menu item at 14North and are very popular; certainly a dish to try if you are visiting the Island!

We're just as passionate about a great drinks offering at 14North. We stock local Apple Orphanage apple juice, Keshal, Roots Bev Co ginger juice and great craft beers both locally sourced from Hooded Ram Brewery and from further afield.

BEETROOT AND GOAT'S CHEESE WITH PICKLED WALNUTS AND APPLE PURÉE

SERVES 4

Ingredients

1 large beetroot
2 tbsp rapeseed oil
4 radishes (quartered)
salt and pepper

Beetroot Sorbet
1 large beetroot
300ml water
300g caster sugar

Beetroot Purée
1 large beetroot
2 tbsp rapeseed oil
salt

Apple Purée
2 Granny Smith apples
50g caster sugar
salt

Goat's Cheese Mousse
300g goat's cheese
1 sprig of thyme
salt and pepper

To Serve
3 pickled walnuts (quartered)
handful of micro salad leaves

Method

Start by boiling all 3 beetroot in salted water for about 45 minutes until tender. Remove from the water, allow to cool and peel the beetroot. Slice 1 beetroot on a mandolin to a 1mm thickness and leave to one side.

For the Beetroot Sorbet
With the second beetroot, make the beetroot sorbet. Dice the beetroot and boil again with 300ml water and 300g caster sugar until the sugar has dissolved. Blend the ingredients until smooth and freeze, removing from the freezer every 20 minutes to mix gently with a fork until frozen.
Preheat oven to 180°C/gas 4

For the Beetroot Purée
The third beetroot is blended in a food processor with 2 tablespoons of rapeseed oil until smooth. Season with salt.

For the Apple Purée
To make the apple purée, peel the Granny Smiths, core and roughly chop. Cook with the 50g sugar and just a splash of water until cooked. Blend until smooth and season.

For the Goat's Cheese Mousse
For the goat's cheese mousse place the goat's cheese in a food processor with 1 sprig of thyme leaves, a splash of hot water and salt and pepper to taste.
Roast the radishes with 2 tablespoons of rapeseed oil, salt and pepper until just cooked. This will take just a few minutes.

To Serve
Once all the ingredients have been prepared you can start to assemble the dish. Lay the sliced beetroot in a line, overlapping slightly. Carefully arrange the apple purée, goat's cheese mousse, pickled walnuts and beetroot purée on and around the sliced beetroot. Garnish the plate with the micro salad leaves and just before serving place a quenelle of the beetroot sorbet on the dish.

LAMB WELLINGTON WITH WILD GARLIC MASH, CARROTS, ROAST CAULIFLOWER AND A CAPER AND TOMATO JUS

SERVES 4

Ingredients

Lamb Wellington

2 canons of lamb (sinew and skin removed, each cut into 2)
1 leek
4 slices Parma ham
2 sheets puff pastry (each cut into 2)
1 egg (for eggwash)
olive oil
salt and pepper

Caper and Tomato Jus

500ml lamb stock
1 tsp redcurrant jelly
1 tomato (peeled, deseeded and chopped into 5cm dice)
3 tsp capers

Wild Garlic Mash, Carrots, Roast Cauliflower

4 large Maris Piper potatoes (peeled and diced)
25g cream
25g butter
1 bunch of wild garlic leaves (washed)
4 medium-sized carrots (peeled and chopped)
2 tbsp Ellerslie Farm rapeseed oil
12 cauliflower florets
olive oil
salt and pepper

Method

For the Lamb Wellington
Preheat oven to 200°C/gas 6

Rub the lamb with olive oil and season with salt and pepper. Seal the lamb in a hot frying pan and remove to cool.

Top and tail the leek, slice down the length of the leek from the centre out. Wash the leek and blanch the sheets of leek in boiling water for 30 seconds and refresh in iced water. Remove from the water and dry. Lay the 4 slices of Parma ham on the kitchen counter. On top of each piece of Parma ham lay the sheets of leek then place the lamb canons on top of the leek. Roll the ham and leeks tightly around the lamb. Roll out the puff pastry so that it is large enough to wrap the lamb parcels in. Carefully roll the lamb in the pastry, sealing the joins with some eggwash, then eggwash the outside of the pastry and leave the Wellingtons to rest in the fridge.

For the Jus
Prepare the jus by reducing the stock by half and adding the redcurrant jelly.

Wild Garlic Mash, Carrots, Roast Cauliflower
Cook the potato in boiling salted water. When cooked, drain and mash. Heat the cream and butter together and add to the potato. Whilst the potatoes are cooking blanch the wild garlic leaves in boiling salted water before cooling them in iced water. Blend the leaves with a stick blender and incorporate into the mashed potato to taste. Season the mash.
Cook the carrots in boiling salted water. When cooked add the rapeseed oil and blend with a stick blender until smooth.
Season the cauliflower with salt and pepper and drizzle with a little olive oil. Place the cauliflower on a tray and

cook for the same amount of time as the Wellingtons.

To Finish

Bake the Wellingtons for about 18 minutes, the pastry
should be golden. Allow to rest for 5 minutes.
Whilst the lamb is resting make sure the other
ingredients are all hot and add the tomato and capers
to the jus. Cut the excess pastry from the Wellingtons
and cut them in half.

To Serve

Start plating by adding the carrot purée and topping it
with the lamb Wellington halves. Add the cauliflower
florets and the garlic mash to the plate. Spoon the jus
around the dish.

PEANUT BUTTER PARFAIT WITH CHOCOLATE ICE CREAM, PEANUT BRITTLE, HONEYCOMB AND CARAMEL SAUCE

SERVES 4

Ingredients

Peanut Butter Parfait
40g caster sugar
20ml water
2 egg yolks
100ml cream
40g smooth peanut butter (warmed slightly)

Peanut Brittle
100g salted peanuts
100g caster sugar
20ml water

Honeycomb
40g caster sugar
12g golden syrup
40g glucose syrup
4g bicarbonate of soda (sieved)

Caramel Sauce
60g butter
100g caster sugar
½ tsp white wine vinegar
15ml water
15ml golden syrup
65ml double cream

Chocolate Ice Cream
We make our own but you can buy your favourite brand for this recipe.

Method

For the Peanut Butter Parfait
Heat the sugar and water to 118°C to form a sugar syrup. To make a sabayon, whisk the egg yolks together in a mixer and then pour the sugar syrup in a slow steady stream over the yolks, whisking continuously at a medium to high speed until the mixture has cooled.
Whisk the cream to form soft peaks and then fold it into the peanut butter before folding this new mixture into the sabayon. Decant this into 4 moulds and freeze for at least 6 hours.

For the Peanut Brittle
Lightly toast the peanuts under a medium grill. Mix the sugar with 20ml of water and heat until a dark golden colour. Once golden add the peanuts and pour the mixture onto a tray to cool. Once cool blend in a food processor until a rough crumb texture.

For the Honeycomb
In a saucepan, heat the sugar along with the golden syrup and glucose syrup until it reaches the colour of straw. Carefully whisk in the bicarbonate of soda and transfer to a tray lined with greaseproof paper. Allow to cool for 10 minutes and then put into the fridge for 1 hour. Store the honeycomb in an airtight container until needed.

For the Caramel Sauce
Boil all the ingredients apart from the cream. When the mixture is dark and thick add the cream and whisk. Allow to cool.

To Serve
Start by placing a swirl of caramel on the plate and put the parfait on top of this. Spoon some of the brittle next to the parfait and top this with a scoop of chocolate ice cream. Break up some honeycomb and place this on the parfait. Serve.

The Island Kitchen : Little Fish Cafe

LITTLE FISH CAFE

31 North Quay, Douglas, Isle of Man IM1 4LB
01624 622518
www.littlefishcafe.com

Little Fish Cafe is the latest addition to the Rock Food Concepts portfolio of hospitality venues, all based within a short walk of one another. Little Fish Cafe opened in April 2014, providing Douglas with a new, vibrant dining option.

Combining freshly caught local seafood, refreshing cocktails and freshly brewed coffee, Little Fish Cafe offers all-day dining with stunning quayside views only a short walk from Douglas town centre.

We believe that great food brings people together and the menu at Little Fish offers something for everyone – whether an intimate candlelit dinner and cocktails, a quick coffee on the go, or lunch in the sun with a group of friends.

Inspired by visits to the seaside, we aim to evoke childhood memories whilst providing customers with quality food and service befitting of a more sophisticated dining experience.

As an island, we are lucky to have some of the most beautiful shellfish in the British Isles; stunning lobsters and crab are caught every day and delivered straight to us – we are also fortunate enough to serve the increasingly well renowned Manx queenies. Alongside our regular menu we always have a rotating specials board showcasing the best of the day's catch.

We work with the freshest possible produce and use simple cooking methods to ensure that every dish is showcased to its full potential. Meaning that the food served at Little Fish Cafe is humble, yet delicious.

But we aren't just passionate about our food. To complement the food we offer carefully selected wines and a dedicated cocktail menu. This allows customers to enjoy the perfect aperitif, a naughty sweet cocktail or simply a refreshing drink in the sunshine.

On weekends we serve a well-established brunch menu throughout the day from classic Eggs Benedict to the more adventurous Queenie Po'Boy. Again our drinks menu aims to please with cold-pressed coffee, iced vanilla lattes and Bloody Marys taking centre stage.

QUEENIES WITH BACON, GARLIC AND CREAM

SERVES 4

Ingredients

4 slices Noa Bakehouse sourdough
3g Staarvey Farm lemon thyme
200g bacon (sliced)
480g Manx queenies
2 shallots (sliced)
1 garlic clove (crushed)
150ml white wine
150ml Isle of Man Creamery double cream
5g Ryehill Farm parsley (chopped)
5g Staarvey Farm micro herbs
Ellerslie Farm rapeseed oil
salt and pepper

Method

Preheat oven to 200°C/gas 6
Place the 4 slices of sourdough on a baking tray. Drizzle the rapeseed oil and rub the thyme over the sourdough. Bake in the oven for 5 minutes.
Whilst the bread is in the oven, fry the bacon in a hot pan, let it start to catch and stick to the pan. Add the queenies and let them caramelise. Add the shallots, garlic and white wine then simmer for 30 seconds. Add the cream and reduce. Season to taste with salt and pepper.
Serve the queenies over the baked sourdough with a pinch of Ryehill Farm chopped parsley and a bunch of Staarvey Farm micro herbs on top.

MANX LOBSTER ROASTED WITH CAFÉ DE PARIS BUTTER

SERVES 4

Ingredients

Café de Paris Butter

200g Isle of Man Creamery salted butter (softened)
1 tsp parsley (chopped)
1 tsp chives (chopped)
1 tsp tarragon (chopped)
1 tsp capers (chopped)
2 anchovies (rinsed and chopped)
1 shallot (diced)
2 tbsp tomato purée
1 garlic clove (crushed)
2 tsp Dijon mustard
1 dash of Madeira or Cognac
½ tsp paprika
4 Manx lobsters

To Serve

Staarvey Farm salad leaves
2 lemons (cut in half, wrapped in muslin and tied)
salt and pepper

Method

For the Café de Paris Butter

Put the softened butter in a bowl and add the parsley, chives, tarragon, capers, anchovies, shallot, tomato purée, garlic, Dijon mustard, Madeira or Cognac and paprika. Mix together well and season with salt and pepper. Leave to stand for 30 minutes, then place the flavoured butter in greaseproof paper, roll into a sausage shape and twist at both ends. Chill in the fridge until needed. Once chilled, remove the butter from its paper and cut into slices 1.5cm thick.

For the Lobster

To prepare the lobster, place them in a pan with rolling, boiling water for 8 minutes. Remove and allow to cool down completely. Remove the claws and split the lobster down the middle. Rinse each half under cold water, washing out all unwanted parts of the lobster. Remove

the tail meat and cut into bite size chunks. Crack the claws open and remove the meat. Fill the half shells with an even mixture of both meats. Place the shells on a baking tray, season with salt and pepper.

To Serve

Preheat oven to 200°C/gas 6
Break up a slice of Café de Paris butter over each half of lobster. Roast in a preheated oven at 200°C for 8–10 minutes, or until the butter caramelises and starts to change colour. Serve with Staarvey Farm leaves and lemon wedges in muslin.

BURNT VANILLA CREAM

SERVES 4

Ingredients

450ml Isle of Man Creamery double cream
1 vanilla pod (split and scraped)
6 egg yolks
60g caster sugar

To Serve
4 raspberries
5g icing sugar
granulated sugar

Method

You will need 2 deep saucepans, a non-metallic bowl that can fit on top of one pan, a balloon whisk, a pouring jug, a sieve, a brûlée gun and 4 ramekins.
In a pan add the cream, vanilla pod and its scrapings then bring to the boil and simmer for 5 minutes or until starting to reduce.
In the other pan add about 1 inch of water and bring to a simmer. In the bowl add the egg yolks and sugar. Place the bowl over the pan with simmering water. Stir continuously, cooking out the egg yolks and sugar until smooth, thick and a pale yellow colour.
Pour the vanilla cream into the thickened egg yolk mixture whilst stirring continuously. Pass through a fine sieve into the pouring jug then into ramekins and leave to set in the fridge for at least 2 hours or until set.

To Serve
When ready to serve, sprinkle a thin, even layer of granulated sugar completely covering the top. Caramelise the sugar with the brûlée gun until a light brown colour. Serve with a fresh raspberry on top and a sprinkle of icing sugar.

DOUGLAS AND THE EAST

COAST

18-22 Loch Promenade, Douglas, Isle of Man IM1 2LX
01624 698800
www.claremonthoteldouglas.com

The Claremont is officially the highest-rated hotel on the Isle of Man, unique in having achieved 4-Star Gold status and offering its guests a refined excellence in both hospitality and cuisine. Located on the promenade at the heart of the Island's capital, Douglas, and situated adjacent to the Island's government buildings, business district, retail area and ferry terminal, the Claremont provides an ideal base for both business and leisure.

Our philosophy is simply 'Excellence as Standard' with opulent rooms that delicately balance modern aesthetics, luxurious comfort and the connectivity requirements of the modern day traveller. With complimentary high-speed Wi-Fi throughout the property, welcoming staff, 24hr business services and featuring the beautiful Coast Bar & Brasserie, the Claremont provides the perfect location.

Centrally located to the Loch Promenade at the heart of Douglas, with stunning panoramic views across the bay and out to sea, Coast Bar & Brasserie is renowned as a first class restaurant where guests can choose from a selection of exquisite dishes full of local Manx produce. Featuring all-day dining and a friendly attentive service, Coast is the perfect location to enjoy breakfast, a two-course express lunch for only £10pp, luxury afternoon tea, or an à la carte dinner.

STEAK TARTARE

SERVES 4

Ingredients

1 x 226g Manx fillet steak (finely diced)
1 tbsp mini capers (finely diced)
1 tbsp gherkins (finely diced)
1 tbsp flat-leaf parley (finely diced)
½ shallot (finely diced)
1 tbsp Dijon mustard
3 tbsp tomato ketchup
1 tsp Worcestershire sauce
1 tsp Tabasco sauce
½ tsp Maldon sea salt
1 ½ tsp white pepper

Method

Mix all the ingredients together and serve with a piece of Noa Bakehouse baguette lightly toasted.

SEA BREAM, KALE CRUSTED POTATOES, CAPERS AND LEMON

SERVES 4

Ingredients

12 new potatoes
250g kale
56g butter
4 sea bream (filleted)
1 lemon
1 tbsp mini capers
1 tbsp flat-leaf parley (finely chopped)
2 tbsp extra virgin olive oil
salt and pepper

Method

Cook the potatoes in a pan of boiling salted water for 20–30 minutes, then add the kale and cook for a further 8–10 minutes. Drain and return to the pan then crush with a fork, add the butter and a pinch of salt and pepper. Pan-fry the bream skin-side down with a little oil for 2 minutes, then place under a hot grill for a further 2 minutes until the fish is cooked. In a small bowl mix the zest and juice of the lemon then add the capers and finely chopped parsley.

The Island Kitchen : Coast

DEEP-FRIED APPLES CRÈME FRAICHE

SERVES 4

Ingredients

4 Granny Smith apples
200ml sparkling water
100g self-raising flour
100g caster sugar
1 tbsp ground cinnamon
crème fraiche

Method

Peel and core the apples. In a bowl mix together the sparkling water and the flour to form a batter then add the apples and deep fry at 180°C for 2–3 minutes until golden brown. Drain onto a piece of kitchen paper and set aside. In another bowl mix together the caster sugar and cinnamon, then add the apples to coat them. Serve with crème fraiche.

DOUGLAS AND THE EAST

TANROAGAN

9 Ridgeway Street, Douglas, Isle of Man IM1 1EW
01624 612355
www.tanroagan.co.uk

Tanroagan, simply translated as Shell (Tan) Scallop (Roagan) from Manx Gaelic, is a family-run restaurant owned by the Mowat family. The restaurant is located a few feet from North Quay, home to Douglas marina and in recent years gaining a deserved reputation as a popular leisure and dining-out destination with artisan markets, café bars and restaurants. Joan and Graham Mowat took over the reins from local chef and fisherman Butch Buttery in April 2006, despite coming to the Island to retire after a lengthy career in hospitality. The following day the restaurant hosted TV celebrities, the Hairy Bikers, and has gone on to welcome many visiting celebrities over the years with the Island being a popular destination for film and tv show productions. However, the real stars at Tanroagan are the many visitors and locals who come time and time again to enjoy the fresh and tastiest seafood found on the Island; particular favourites being local Manx lobsters, scallops and queenies.

Located in the middle of the Irish Sea it is no wonder the Isle of Man boasts some of the very best fish and seafood in the British Isles. Famous locally and around the world for its delicious Manx scallops, queenies and lobsters, the Island has become an established destination for foodies looking for a great culinary experience as well as enjoying the fantastic scenery, activities and heritage the Isle of Man has to offer. A massive boost to the culinary experience has been the growth of small independent food and drink producers, allowing restaurants like Tanroagan to offer diners a true taste of the Island through dishes incorporating produce and ingredients sourced here on the Island.

To keep up with the food revolution taking place on the Island we gave Tanroagan a complete makeover in November 2013, bringing the restaurant in line with our then recently opened Boatyard Restaurant. A brand new entrance with ceiling-to-floor windows, patio doors and a contemporary facade now welcomes you when arriving at Tanroagan. The time-worn and creaky wooden floor boards have been replaced by a beautiful Spanish tiled floor with built in underfloor heating, essential throughout the Manx wintery months. Featured lighting, driftwood tables and candlelit tables combine to create a vibrant and exciting dining experience.

There is simply no better place to experience Manx sourced cuisine and the delights of the sea than at Tanroagan, the Island's long established and only specialist seafood restaurant, where fresh seafood really is the dish of the day.

LOBSTER AND FISH FRITTERS

SERVES 4

Ingredients

100g plain flour
20g cornflour
large pinch baking powder
1 shallot (finely diced)
1 tbsp fresh coriander (chopped)
1 large fresh chilli (deseeded and finely chopped)
250g lobster meat and white fish (cut into small cubes)
200ml water
oil for frying
salt and pepper

To Serve
sweet chilli dipping sauce

Method

Mix the flour, cornflour and baking powder with the water until smooth.
Add in all the other ingredients and season.
Heat a frying pan, add some oil and spoon small amounts of the mixture into the pan. Cook on one side, flip and cook on the other, then turn the heat down and allow to cook through.
Serve with sweet chilli dipping sauce.

MANX QUEENIE PIE WITH LEEK AND BACON BEURRE BLANC AND SAMPHIRE

SERVES 4

Ingredients

Cheese Pastry

340g plain Laxey flour
170g Isle of Man Creamery butter
85g Manx vintage Cheddar (grated)
2 Gellings egg yolks (plus 1 for making an eggwash)
1 tbsp poppy seeds
2 tbsp cold water
salt
baking beans for blind baking

Beurre Blanc

4 rashers of streaky bacon
1 tbsp Manx rapeseed oil /olive oil mix
1 small onion (finely chopped)
1 clove garlic (crushed)
1 small leek, white part only (finely chopped)
350ml white wine (reduced to half)
150ml Isle of Man Creamery double cream
56g Isle of Man Creamery butter (cold, small cubes)
salt and pepper

Filling

Manx queenies, depending on the size of your mini pie dishes approx 85g per tart tin
1 tbsp Manx rapeseed oil /olive oil mix
salt and pepper

To Serve

200g samphire

Method

For the Cheese Pastry

Preheat oven to 190°C/gas 5
In a food processor blitz the plain flour, cold butter and a pinch of salt until they have the appearance of fine breadcrumbs.
Add the grated Manx vintage Cheddar, the egg yolks, poppy seeds and 2 tbsp of cold water, then blitz until the mixture all comes together. Take the pastry out and flatten slightly then wrap in cling film and chill for at least 30 minutes. The pastry can be frozen at this point is you are making ahead of time.
Once chilled take the pastry out of the fridge, roll out and cut to fit your tart tin. Roll out another larger circle of pastry for your pie top and set aside. Blind bake your tart at 190°C for 9 minutes, then take out your baking beans and make sure the pastry is cooked before egg-washing with an egg yolk. Put the pastry back into the oven and cook until it is golden brown, then set aside.

For the Beurre Blanc

Whilst the pastry is cooking make some crispy streaky bacon. Cut the bacon into small pieces, sauté until crisp, drain well and set aside.
Put a tablespoon of mixed Manx rapeseed oil and olive oil in a small saucepan to warm. Add the chopped onion, crushed garlic and leek and cook gently until soft but without colouring.
Add reduced wine and the double cream, bring up to just under boiling point and whisk in the cold butter in small cubes. Cook until the butter is absorbed, but do not boil. Add the crispy bacon and taste for seasoning. Put to one side.

For the Filling

Preheat oven to 200°C/gas 6
In a frying pan heat the rapeseed and olive oil mix until a haze forms. Lightly season the queenies and add to the hot pan; just let the queenies colour and then remove from the heat.
Fill the glazed pie cases to the top with queenies then

spoon over the leek and bacon beurre blanc to halfway, setting aside any remaining sauce and keeping warm. Dampen the edge of the pastry case and put the pastry top on and seal. Trim the edge and eggwash the top, making a slit in the top to allow steam to escape.

Place the pie in the oven and cook until a light golden brown. Approx 9 minutes.

Remove from the oven and leave to rest.

To Serve

Bring a pan of salted water to the boil. Add the samphire and cook for 3 minutes, drain and arrange on a serving plate.

Carefully remove the pie from the tin and place on the samphire. Pour the remaining beurre blanc around the pie.

Tip

When making the cheese pastry, local wild garlic seeds or fennel seeds could be used instead of the poppy seeds. Everything can be prepared ahead of time up to cooking the queenies.

CHOCOLATE AND BEETROOT BROWNIES
SERVES 4

Ingredients

200g butter
300g dark chocolate
3 eggs
250g caster sugar
120g beetroot (cooked and puréed)
90g plain flour

To Serve
vanilla ice cream
chocolate sauce

Method

Preheat oven to 160°C/gas 3

Line a 30cm x 18cm (11in x 7in approx.) baking tin with baking parchment.
Melt the butter and chocolate either on low power in a microwave (checking often to avoid burning the chocolate), or in a bowl over a pan of simmering water (making sure that the water does not touch the bowl). Beat the eggs and sugar until light and creamy in a mixer. Stir in the melted chocolate and butter, then add the beetroot purée and fold in the flour. Pour the mixture into the prepared baking tin and bake for approx 25–30 minutes, depending on your oven. Test by inserting a skewer into the cooked brownie, it should come out clean. If the skewer comes out sticky cook the brownie for a few more minutes.

To Serve
Serve with vanilla ice cream and warm chocolate sauce.

HAWORTHS

Regency Hotel, Queens Promenade, Douglas, Isle of Man, IM2 4NN
01624 663553
www.haworths.im

Located on the ground floor of The Regency Hotel, the elegant restaurant and its intimate bar are ideal surroundings to experience Carl's food.

A combination of traditional and modernity, in muted tones with panoramic sea views, oak-panelled walls and generously spaced immaculately dressed tables, the restaurant can cater for up to 60 diners and is a wonderful location for a wedding. Haworths also boasts a supremely comfortable exclusive private dining room for up to 20 guests where privacy and intimacy is guaranteed, and menus can be created to suit each individual customer's taste.

Carl takes full advantage of all the wonderful produce the Island has to offer and works closely with local growers and suppliers to guarantee that the produce is at its seasonal best. The menu changes daily, offering dishes to suit all tastes from hotel residents to local people wanting to celebrate that special occasion. From the homemade crisps and breads to start your meal, to the petit fours of truffles and fudge, all the food is produced by the kitchen team.

Whatever the dish you choose it is always geared around quality ingredients

and attentive cooking.

From bespoke menus and 8-course tasting menus to Manx fillet steak, all tastes and requirements are catered for and are all treated with the same care and attention.

The food is complemented with an exciting modern wine list featuring New World wines as well as some European classics.

With his wife Renee at the Front of House, her attention to detail working alongside her friendly and professional team, this restaurant is very much becoming a destination for both the discerning traveller and local alike.

CALL 694 694
ConisterBank
36
Local Businesses
ConisterBank

THE REGENCY HOTEL

CRAB AND LOBSTER SALAD, CRAB BEIGNETS, CHILLED TOMATO JUICE

SERVES 4

Ingredients

Tomato Juice

500g ripe vine tomatoes
1 sheet of leaf gelatine
salt and pepper

Crab Salad

50g white crab meat
50g lobster meat (diced)
5g shallots (finely chopped)
10g tomato and cucumber (skinned, deseeded and finely diced)
5g radish (cut into fine strips)
6 tarragon leaves
20g mayonnaise
juice of ¼ Lime
¼ tsp chives (chopped)
3 slices of cooked lobster tail meat
salt and pepper

Crab Beignets

50g choux pastry
50g white crab meat
pinch of cayenne pepper
2 tsp lime juice

To Serve

salad leaves

Method

For the Tomato Juice

Liquidise the tomatoes and freeze.
Place the frozen tomatoes in a muslin cloth over a bowl and allow to defrost slowly, retaining the liquid which passes through the muslin.

Place the liquid in a pan and, over a medium heat, reduce slowly until you have 300ml. Season to taste.
Place the gelatine sheets in cold water to soak, remove the gelatine from the water and squeeze off the excess water. Dissolve the gelatine in the tomato juice then place in a container and put in the fridge to slowly set.

For the Crab Salad

Leaving out the lobster tail meat, gently fold all the remaining ingredients together, making sure that everything is well mixed. Place in the fridge until needed.

For the Crab Beignets

Mix all the ingredients together.
Roll the mixture into small balls approx 2cm in diameter
Place them in a deep fat fryer at 180°C until they are golden brown, place on kitchen paper to absorb any excess oil.

To Serve

Arrange the crab mixture in the centre of a serving plate and place the sliced lobster meat along the middle of the crab salad. Lightly break up the tomato jelly and arrange around the crab salad. Place the hot crab beignets next to the lobster tail and finally garnish with a few salad leaves.

LOIN AND BREAST OF MANX LAMB, AUBERGINE PURÉE AND BOULANGIERE POTATOES

SERVES 4

Ingredients

Lamb Loin

300g lamb loin
100g chicken breast
30g egg white
50g double cream
pinch rosemary (chopped)
10g crisp bread croutons
50g caul fat
salt and pepper

Breast of Lamb

1kg lamb breast
100g carrots, onion, leek, celery (all finely diced)
2 cloves garlic
2 sprigs of rosemary and thyme
1 bay leaf
50g tomato purée
200ml red wine
2 ltr lamb stock
salt and pepper

Aubergine Purée

1 aubergine
30ml cream
30g butter
salt and pepper

Boulangiere Potatoes

500g onions (sliced)
20g butter
fresh thyme
1kg potatoes (peeled)
500ml lamb stock
salt and pepper

To Serve

lamb stock
red wine
rosemary

Method

For the Lamb Loin

Season the lamb loin and seal in very hot oil until a light golden colour, place on kitchen paper to absorb any excess oil and place in the fridge.

In the meantime, blitz the chicken in a food processor with the egg white and a good pinch of salt until the chicken becomes a smooth paste. Gently fold in the cream until it has all absorbed into the chicken. Finally, fold in the rosemary and croutons. Place the mousse in the fridge for a minimum of 1 hour.

Wash the caul fat under running cold water, pat dry and lay out flat on a chopping board.

Spread some of the mousse, in a rectangular shape, in the middle of the caul fat, place the lamb loin on top of the mousse, then spread more of the mousse on the top of the lamb.

Gently fold the caul fat over the lamb loin so that the whole of the loin is covered in mousse.

Place the lamb in the fridge until required.

For the Breast of Lamb

Preheat oven to 120°C/gas ½

Season the lamb breast and place flat in a roasting tray, cover with the vegetables, garlic and herbs. Add the tomato purée and wine, and add enough stock so that the breast is completely covered.

Cover with tinfoil and place in the oven at 120°C for approx. 2½ hrs. Remove the breast from the cooking liquor, place on a flat tray, weight down the breast so that it is pressed then place in fridge and leave to cool.

The Island Kitchen : Haworths

For the Aubergine Purée

Place the aubergine directly onto an open flame, turning regularly so that there is even charring and cooking all over the aubergine.

Allow to cool then remove all the charred skin. Purée the flesh, place in a saucepan with the cream and butter, mix well and season. Set aside.

For the Boulangiere Potatoes

Preheat oven to 150°C / gas 2

Sweat the onions in the butter with a good pinch of thyme until well cooked. Season to taste.

Thinly slice the potatoes.

Arrange the sliced potatoes on the base of a ovenproof dish, cover the potatoes with onions, then repeat with the potatoes and onions until all the onions have been used, finishing with a layer of potatoes.

Pour in the lamb stock until it reaches just below the top of the potatoes.Cover the dish with foil and bake at 150°C until the potatoes are well cooked.

To Finish

Preheat oven to 180°C / gas 4

Heat up a little oil and butter in a frying pan, add the loin of lamb and cook, turning often, until the lamb is an even golden brown colour. Place in a hot oven at 180°C for 12 minutes. Remove from the oven and allow to rest for a minimum of 3 minutes before slicing.

Cut the breast of lamb into squares of approx. 4cm.

Place in the pan and fry until lightly coloured, then put in the oven to reheat.

Cut out a portion of potatoes and reheat in the oven.

To Serve

Reheat the aubergine purée, and place on a serving plate. Slice the lamb loin, arrange on the plate and garnish with the boulangiere potatoes and lamb breast. Finish with a jus of lamb stock reduced with red wine and rosemary.

HONEY PARFAIT, CHOCOLATE SORBET, THYME SCENTED BISCUITS

SERVES 4

Ingredients

Honey Parfait
100g caster sugar
2 egg yolks
4 eggs
150g Manx honey
200ml double cream

Chocolate Sorbet
150g chocolate
75g cocoa powder
250g caster sugar
500ml water

Thyme Scented Biscuits
50g icing sugar
50g butter
50g egg white
50g plain flour
½ tsp fresh thyme leaves

Method

For the Honey Parfait
Put the sugar in a pan with a little water and cook to 118°C (or until it reaches the soft ball stage). Meanwhile put the yolks and eggs in a mixing bowl and whisk until the mixture thickens. Slowly pour in the cooked sugar and continue whisking slowly until the mixture has cooled. Gently fold the honey into the mixture, lightly whip the cream and fold this into the honey mixture.
Pour into moulds and place in the freezer.

For the Chocolate Sorbet
Place all the ingredients into a pan, mix well and cook slowly until the chocolate has dissolved.

Pass through a sieve and allow to cool.
Place in an ice cream machine and churn until it reaches the required consistency.

For the Thyme Scented Biscuits
Preheat oven to 180°C/gas 4
Cream the sugar and butter, mix in the egg white, then fold in the flour to make a paste.
Place in the fridge for a minimum of 1 hour.
Spread the mixture on a baking tray into the required shape. Sprinkle a few thyme leaves on top of each of the biscuits.
Place in the hot oven at 180°C and cook until a light golden brown.
Remove from the tray and allow to cool.

ENZO'S

52 Bucks Rd, Douglas, IM1 3AD
01624 622653
www.facebook.com/Enzos-Restaurant-447954141951669

Enzo's is a cosy restaurant in Bucks Road, Douglas serving modern cuisine with an Italian twist. Our extensive menu showcases an excellent variety of dishes made using local produce and the freshest ingredients; everything is made on the premises, including our desserts and tasty dairy ice cream. A comprehensive wine list complements the choice of dishes and Enzo's is well renowned for their prompt service.

Head Chef at Enzo's, Stuart Fenney, qualified at St Helens College catering school, and gained a diploma in Professional Cookery. He moved to the Isle of Man in 2006 and, after experience in the hotel industry, worked in various restaurants eventually taking the post of Head Chef at Enzo's in 2013.

At Enzo's, in the heart of Douglas, you will find a restaurant able to cater for any occasion with the upmost professional manner.

HOMEMADE CRAB AND LOBSTER RAVIOLI, SAUCE THERMIDOR

SERVES 4

Ingredients

Pasta
350g plain strong flour
3 eggs
5 egg yolks
1 egg (beaten with water as an eggwash)
salt and pepper

Filling
1 large lobster (cooked)
250g mixed crab meat
chives (freshly chopped)
salt and pepper

Sauce Thermidor
50g butter
2 shallots (chopped)
30ml brandy
50ml white wine
1 tsp Dijon mustard
vegetable stock
50ml fresh cream
Gruyère cheese (grated)

Method

For the Ravioli
Mix the flour, eggs and egg yolks to make a dough then rest it for an hour in the fridge. Once chilled, roll the dough through a pasta machine forming it into sheets. Mix the chopped lobster meat with the crab meat and chives, and season with salt and pepper. Lay out a pasta sheet and place the meat mixture onto the sheet in intervals, brush the sheet with eggwash and cover with another pasta sheet. Using a round 10cm cutter, shape the ravioli and close firmly at the edges. Repeat until all the pasta and lobster mix is used up.
Boil the ravioli in about 2 litres of boiling water for 5 minutes.

For the Sauce Thermidor
In the meantime, to make the sauce, put a saucepan on the stove, melt the butter over a medium heat, add the shallots and cook until translucent.
Add the brandy and flame it, then add the wine and reduce down.
Next add the mustard and vegetable stock to the sauce and reduce again. Finally, finish the sauce by adding the cream and Gruyère cheese.

To Serve
Place the cooked ravioli on a plate and cover with the thermidor sauce.

RACK OF MANX LAMB, DAUPHOINOISE POTATOES, PORT WINE JUS

SERVES 4

Ingredients

1 x 4 sticks rack of lamb (French trimmed)

Dauphinoise Potatoes
4 potatoes (peeled and washed)
2 shallots (chopped)
2 cloves garlic (chopped)
100ml fresh cream
salt and pepper

Crust
100g fresh breadcrumbs
parsley (chopped)
thyme (chopped)
olive oil
salt and pepper

Jus
shallots (chopped)
butter
port wine
beef stock
salt and pepper

Method

For the Dauphinoise Potatoes
Preheat oven to 200°C/gas 6
Slice the potatoes very thinly, then place on a baking tray sprinkling with the chopped shallots and garlic, and season with salt and pepper. Cover the potatoes with the fresh cream then bake in the oven for about 1½ hours until cooked.

For the Crust
Place the breadcrumbs in a mixing bowl and mix in the chopped parsley and thyme. Add salt, pepper and a little olive oil, mixing together to form a smooth paste.
Now cook the rack of lamb in a hot frying pan until it is roasted and coloured on both sides. Put the breadcrumb crust on the fatty side and pat it until it is firm.
Place the rack of lamb in the oven for about 15 minutes at 200°C to cook it until pink.
If the potatoes are ready, take out of the oven and allow to cool down, then cut and shape with a round cutter.

For the Jus
Place chopped shallots and butter in a saucepan, fry gently and add the port wine, reduce the liquid then add the beef stock and season with salt and pepper. Simmer for approx 10 minutes.

To Serve
Once the rack of lamb is cooked, rest it on a chopping board for 4 minutes then cut through the sticks. Place the dauphinoise potatoes on a serving plate, gently lean over the lamb sticks and pour the sauce over.

FRESH BERRIES PAVLOVA

SERVES 4

Ingredients

Meringue
3 egg whites
100g caster sugar

Raspberry Sauce
250g fresh raspberries
100g caster sugar
100ml water

Chantilly Cream
250ml fresh double cream
1 tbsp icing sugar
1 tsp vanilla essence

To Serve
150g mixed fresh berries

Method

For the Meringue
Prepare overnight the day before serving.
Preheat oven to 150°C/gas 2
Using an electric whisk, whisk the egg whites while gradually adding the sugar until stiff peaks form. Place the contents in a piping bag and pipe onto a baking tray covered with parchment paper. Bake in the oven for about an hour and leave the meringues in the oven, switched off, overnight.

For the Raspberry Sauce
Place the raspberries, sugar and water in a saucepan, bring to the boil and cook for about 3 minutes.
Remove the contents from the saucepan and place in a blender. Carefully blend until it becomes liquid.
Sieve the contents into a bowl with a fine strainer.

For the Chantilly Cream
Place all ingredients in a mixing bowl and mixed until the cream holds medium soft peaks.

To Serve
Gently place 2 tablespoons of crème Chantilly onto the meringue, add the fresh berries and cover with the raspberry sauce.

SAMPHIRE RESTAURANT AND BISTRO

Samphire Restaurant & Bistro, 35 North Quay, Douglas IM1 4LB
01624 617093
www.facebook.com: Samphire Restaurant Bistro

At Samphire we strive to showcase how special simplicity can be. Our vision is to bring to the Island the highest quality informal dining experience that is the equal of anything you might find in any major city. The huge advantage we have over city dining, however, is the vast array of fresh, local produce that arrives daily. Provenance is everything to us. As is quality and freshness.

Our menu is displayed daily on our large blackboard and whilst regulars will notice a few favourite staple dishes, we change the menu daily according to availability, freshness and season.

At Samphire, the food is everything, combined with a wine list that is as unique to the Island as it is affordable. We are blessed to have such an array of fresh, local meat, fish, shellfish, game and vegetables. That said, we are not shy about bringing you the best of the rest – whether that be imported French cheeses, oysters, clams and mussels from around the north-west coast of England or charcuterie from long established, passionate and trusted Italian suppliers.

Head Chef, Richard Birch, and his small team have deservedly earned the top reputation that is responsible for filling Samphire everyday. Our customers provide the ambience and the buzz in our beautiful harbourside location – as stunning in winter with the high tides lapping over the quayside as it is glorious in summer – every changing scene framed in our huge picture windows that provide the perfect screen for people, boat and weather watching!

We are proud to be a small part of an ever-growing Manx food scene that has blossomed over the recent past. The North Quay dining cluster is leading the way and we look forward to welcoming you to the simplicity of Samphire.

SMOKED SALMON SCOTCH EGG

SERVES 4

Ingredients

4 large eggs
300g Manx smoked salmon
1 egg yolk
1 shallot (finely chopped)
2 sprigs of dill
juice of 1 lemon
white pepper

Breadcrumbs
100g plain flour
2 large eggs (beaten)
200g breadcrumbs

Tartar Sauce
50g capers (finely chopped)
50g gherkins (finely chopped)
1 shallot (finely chopped)
2 sprig of dill (finely chopped)
2 sprigs of flat-leaf parsley (finely chopped)
1 hard boiled egg (chopped)
juice of ½ lemon
100g mayonnaise

To Serve
rocket and fennel salad

Method

Bring a pan of water to the boil and place 4 large eggs into the pan for 6 minutes, strain and refresh, then de-shell the eggs and set aside.
Place the smoked salmon, egg yolk, shallot and dill into a blender. Blend for 1 minute until smooth, then add the lemon juice and white pepper to taste.
Divide the smoked salmon mixture into 4 and mould around each egg (with slightly wet hands). Place in the fridge to chill for 30 minutes.
Whilst the eggs are chilling prepare 100g of flour, 2 beaten eggs and 200g breadcrumbs on separate trays.

To assemble the Scotch eggs firstly flour the smoked salmon egg, then brush with the beaten eggs and then roll in the breadcrumbs. Deep fry at 170°C for 5 minutes.

For the Tartar Sauce
In a bowl add the finely chopped capers, gherkins, shallot, dill, flat-leaf parsley, and the chopped hard boiled egg along with the juice of ½ lemon to 100g of mayonnaise and mix.

To Serve
Serve the Scotch eggs with a rocket and fennel salad and the tartar sauce

PAN-FRIED FILLET OF COD WITH SAFFRON AND LEEK RISOTTO AND CHORIZO

SERVES 4

Ingredients

250ml white wine
1 large pinch of saffron
700ml chicken stock
½ medium onion (finely chopped)
2 cloves garlic (finely chopped)
226g Arborio rice
1 leek (diced)
1 large knob of butter
150g grated Parmesan cheese
4 x 226g cod fillets

To Serve

a handful of Staarvey Farm pea shoots
200g cooked chorizo (diced)
olive oil

Method

Preheat oven to 200°C/gas 6
Add the white wine and saffron to 600ml of the chicken stock, bring to the boil then simmer. In a separate pan slowly sweat the onion and garlic until translucent, then add the Arborio rice and a ladle of stock. Keep stirring, slowly adding the stock a ladle at a time, letting each ladleful be absorbed before adding the next, until all the stock has been used. Chill on a flat tray for 10 minutes. Pan-fry the diced leek in butter until soft. Next add the cooked risotto rice to the leeks and add the remaining 100ml of chicken stock plus 100g of the Parmesan cheese. Place in a non-stick pan and stir until the mixture reaches a firm, but soft, consistency.
Pan-fry the cod fillet (skin-side down) for 5 minutes, flip over and place in the oven at 200°C for 8 minutes.

To Serve

Place the risotto on a serving plate and lay the cod on top. Garnish with pea shoots, the remaining Parmesan cheese, diced chorizo and a drizzle of good quality olive oil.

TARTE TATIN

SERVES 4

Ingredients

10g butter
200g soft brown sugar
7 Granny Smith apples (peeled and cored)
320g packet of puff pastry
1 egg (beaten)

To Serve

Davison's vanilla ice cream
seasonal fruits

Method

Preheat oven to 200°C/gas 6

Place the sugar in a dry non-stick pan, and melt over a medium heat with the butter until the sugar is dissolved. Carefully place the melted sugar mixture into 4 blini pans. Quarter the apples, piling them up into each pan. Place into a 200°C oven for 10 minutes until the apples are slightly cooked. Take out of the oven and leave to cool for 30 minutes.

Roll out the puff pastry to a £1 coin thickness and cut to the size of the blini pans. Place over the apples and tuck into sides then eggwash with the beaten egg. Place in the oven at 200°C for 10 minutes or until golden brown.

To Serve

Turn out and serve with Davison's vanilla ice cream and seasonal fruits.

NEW MANILA

Queens Promenade, Douglas, Isle of Man IM2 4NH
01624 660600
newmanila.co.uk

Building on many years of experienced and unrivalled reputation, we are one of the best authentic Thai restaurants on the Isle of Man.

New Manila serves Thai cuisine prepared according to ancient recipes collected by proprietor Melody Crosby during her many years of travel in the Far East, with a focus on how the flavours and textures of premium-quality ingredients interact together. Customers can either enjoy their meal in our fully licensed restaurant or use our takeaway service when preferring to eat at home. All our food is cooked to order by our three talented Thai chefs, who pride themselves on serving only the finest and freshest ingredients cooked to a consistently high standard.

THAI SCALLOP SALAD

SERVES 4

Ingredients

Seafood Sauce
3 bird's eye chillies
5 cloves garlic
2 stalks coriander
1 tbsp palm sugar
5 tbsp lime juice

Scallop Salad
1kg scallops
2 tbsp fish sauce
5 tbsp lime juice
1 tbsp palm sugar
3 stalks lemon grass (thinly sliced)
1 red onion (thinly sliced)
1 red pepper (thinly sliced)
1 green pepper (thinly sliced)

Method

For the Seafood Sauce
Place all the ingredients in a blender and mix well. Set aside to use later.

For the Scallop Salad
Boil some water in a large pan. Cook the scallops quickly in the water, about 2 minutes should be sufficient, mix them together then drain and set aside in a large bowl. In another bowl add the fish sauce, lime juice, palm sugar and the seafood sauce then stir them all together and set aside.
Finally, quickly grill the scallops then add to the bowl of ingredients along with the lemon grass, red onion, and red and green peppers and mix well again.
Serve and enjoy.

STEAMED SEABASS WITH GARLIC, CHILLIES AND LIME JUICE
SERVES 4

Ingredients

5 fresh limes
3 tbsp garlic (finely chopped)
bunch of coriander (chopped)
4 long red chillies
1 tbsp palm sugar
3 tbsp fish sauce
2 sides of seabass (filleted)
pinch of ginger (thinly sliced)
bunch of spring onions (sliced) [

Method

Squeeze four limes, chop the garlic and coriander and slice the chillies. Set these aside in separate dishes. The finer you chop chillies the spicier the sauce will be, use 3 or 4 long red chillies and if you want the hotter ones use bird's eye chillies.

Stir together the palm sugar, fish sauce and lime juice in a bowl. Add the garlic and chillies and stir well. Do not add the chopped coriander until just before serving so it stays nice and fresh. Let the mixture sit and marinate for 10 minutes, which is just about enough time to steam the fish.

Lay the fish on an ovenproof plate that will allow a little space all around once it is in the steamer. Steam the fish with thinly sliced ginger for about 5 to 10 minutes, then check how it's doing. It is done when you can pick the fish away from the plate at the thickest portion.

In Thailand, we serve fish like this on a special metal platter that has a little charcoal fire under it to keep the fish warm, but it can be kept warm on a plain platter instead.
Serve immediately while the fish is still hot. Transfer the fish to the serving platter and pour over all the juice that was left on the cooking plate.

Add the chopped coriander to the sauce and stir it up well, then top the fish with about half of it. Slice the remaining lime and place it, as a garnish, on top of the fish along with the sliced spring onions.

To Serve
Serve immediately with hot steamed rice.

THE BEACH – THAI COCONUT BANANA FRITTERS

SERVES 4

Ingredients

Caramel Sauce
200g brown sugar
125ml pouring cream
100g butter (chopped)

Banana Fritters
300g self-raising flour
½ tsp bicarbonate of soda
500ml soda water
85g desiccated coconut
plain flour, to coat
oil for frying
3 large bananas (peeled and thickly sliced)
pure icing sugar, to dust

Method

Preparation time 15 minutes, to cook 15 minutes.

For the Caramel Sauce
To make the caramel sauce, stir the sugar, cream and butter in a saucepan over medium heat for 4–5 minutes or until smooth.

For the Banana Fritters
Sift the self-raising flour and bicarbonate of soda into a bowl. Whisk in the soda water until smooth.
Next spread the coconut and plain flour over separate plates.
Heat the oil in a medium saucepan over a medium heat to 180°C.
Roll 3 pieces of banana in the plain flour and shake off excess. Dip in batter, then roll in the coconut to coat. Carefully add to the oil. Cook for 1–2 minutes or until golden. Transfer to a plate lined with paper towel. Repeat, in 3 more batches, with the remaining banana, flour, batter and coconut.

To Serve
Dust the fritters with icing sugar. Serve with the caramel sauce and vanilla ice cream.

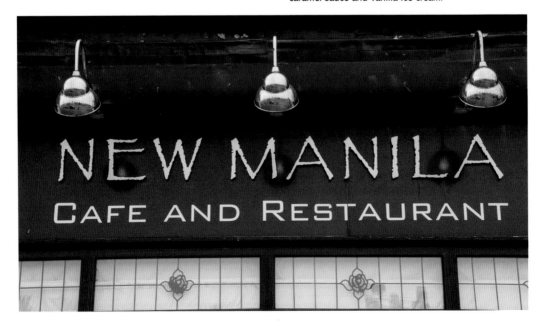

MACFARLANE'S

24 Duke Street, Douglas, Isle of Man, IM1 2AY
01624 624777
www.macfarlanes.im

Since opening in July 2007, Macfarlane's restaurant has firmly established itself as having a reputation for offering the best in local seafood, and Manx beef and lamb. Macfarlane's is also known for its mouth-watering desserts and ice creams. All food is created under the supervision of chef/patron Roy Macfarlane, from Tarbert, Loch Fyne, Argyll in the west of Scotland.

Macfarlane's strives to make sure that your visit to our restaurant is a memorable one for all the right reasons, with the firm belief that 'you're only ever as good as your last meal'.

CASHEL BLUE CHEESE SOUFFLÉ, PETIT SALAD AND BALSAMIC DRESSING

SERVES 4

Ingredients

30g unsalted butter
57g gluten-free plain flour
284ml full-fat milk (heated)
226g Cashel blue cheese
4 organic Manx eggs (separated)
salt and ground white pepper to taste

To Serve
dressed local leaves
aged balsamic dressing
6–8 ramekins lined with butter and grated Parmesan cheese

Method

Preheat oven to 170°C (fan)/gas 5

Sweat the butter over a low heat in a saucepan, then add the flour and cook for a few minutes. Next gradually add the hot milk. Once all the milk has been added and the sauce has thickened slightly add the blue cheese, remembering to stir continually until the sauce is smooth and thick. Now set aside to cool.

After 10 minutes add the egg yolks to the mixture then transfer to a large bowl.

In a separate bowl whisk the egg whites to a soft peak, then fold into the cheese mixture.

Divide into ramekins and bake in a bain-marie in the preheated oven for approx. 30–35 minutes.

Remove from the oven and serve with dressed local leaves and aged balsamic dressing.

The Island Kitchen : Macfarlane's

MANX FISH PIE

SERVES 4

Ingredients

6 large dry Manx potatoes (peeled and roughly chopped)
200g butter
3 free-range egg yolks
85g Manx plain flour
568ml milk
500g vintage Manx Cheddar (grated, plus extra to top the pie)
1 fillet smoked haddock
1 salmon or trout fillet
3 fillets line-caught Manx pollock
226g Manx queenies

To Serve
28g parsley (finely chopped)

Method

Preheat oven to 200°C/gas 6
Boil the potatoes until cooked, drain well then add 85g of the butter and the egg yolks, mash and set aside.
To make the sauce for the pie, sweat the remaining butter with the flour, then add 284ml of the milk and finally the cheese. Season to taste then set aside.
Chop up the fish, but not the queenies, into big chunks, poach and simmer in a heavy-based saucepan for 10 minutes with the remaining 284ml of milk, until half cooked.
Drain off the fish, keeping the milk set aside for the final dish.
Place the fish in a baking dish, cover with the sauce and the remaining milk from the poached fish, add the queenies and pipe the mash on top. Finally top with grated vintage Manx Cheddar.
Bake in the oven for 15–20 minutes until golden brown .
Once ready to serve add freshly chopped parsley.

GLUTEN-FREE CHOCOLATE FONDANT WITH ORANGE AND CHOCOLATE CHIP ICE CREAM

SERVES 4

Ingredients

Chocolate Fondant

125g dark chocolate (70% cocoa solids, chopped)
125g unsalted butter
2 large eggs
2 large egg yolks
4 level dessertspoons caster sugar
2 level tsp gluten-free plain flour

4 lined dariole moulds

Ice Cream

85g dark chocolate
225ml double cream
225ml full-fat milk
1 large orange (zested and juiced)
1 vanilla pod
7 large egg yolks
170g caster sugar
2 tbsp Grand Marnier

To Serve

good quality cocoa powder

Method

For the Chocolate Fondant

Place the chocolate and butter together in a bowl over gently simmering water, making sure that the bowl does not touch the water, and melt slowly. Once melted set aside to cool slightly.
Next crack the whole eggs and the egg yolks into a mixing bowl containing the sugar, add the chocolate mix and the gluten-fee flour, and gently mix together – you don't want too much air in the mixture.
Once combined, transfer to the 4 lined dariole moulds. Refrigerate until required.

For the Ice Cream

Melt the chocolate in a bowl over simmering water, again making sure that the bowl does not touch the water, then spread onto baking parchment and place in the fridge to set.
Put the cream, milk, orange zest, juice and scraped vanilla pod in a saucepan, then gently bring to the boil.
Whisk the egg yolks and sugar over a bain-marie until doubled in volume, stir in half of the cream mix, then transfer back to the cream pan for 30 seconds, removed from the heat. Set aside for a few minutes, pass through a sieve then add the Grand Marnier.
Once cooled place in the fridge.
When properly chilled, break up the cold chocolate and start churning, remembering to add broken chocolate pieces into each layer of ice cream, freeze until ready to serve.

To Serve

Preheat oven to 180°C/gas 4
Cook the fondant at 180°C for approx. 12 minutes. They should be cooked on the outside but soft to touch in the middle. Once ready set aside for 5 minutes to rest, then gently turn out, top with orange chocolate chip ice cream, dust with fine cocoa powder and serve.

The Island Kitchen : Macfarlane's

PORTOFINO RESTAURANT

Portofino Restaurant, 1 Bridge Road, Quay West, Douglas, Isle of Man IM1 5AG
01624 617755
www.portofino.im

Mario Ciappelli arrived on the Isle of Man at the age of 14, starting his career at the Palace Hotel before returning to Italy to complete his training, gaining his Diploma in Hospitality and Catering in Turin. After working on cruise ships for three years, travelling around the world and the Caribbean, he returned to the Island to settle down and in 1989 opened his first restaurant, Ciappelli's. After six years the time was right to move on and he opened The Max restaurant at the King Edward Bay Golf and Country Club in Onchan before retiring for a few years to concentrate on family life. Moving back into his career Mario, along with his brother Enzo, opened La Cucina Restaurant in Bucks Road, Douglas.

Purchasing the site for a new restaurant at the prestigious Quay West, Mario put his heart and soul into his next new venture, Portofino, which opened late in 2010. Located in a fantastic position looking out over the stunning Douglas marina, the modern building houses a stylish interior, which creates a relaxed atmosphere for fine dining. Using the highest quality local produce Mario creates mouth-watering dishes that are sure to impress. Appearing in the Michelin guide for the past three years, Portofino specialises in the finest seafood, Mediterranean and international cuisine.

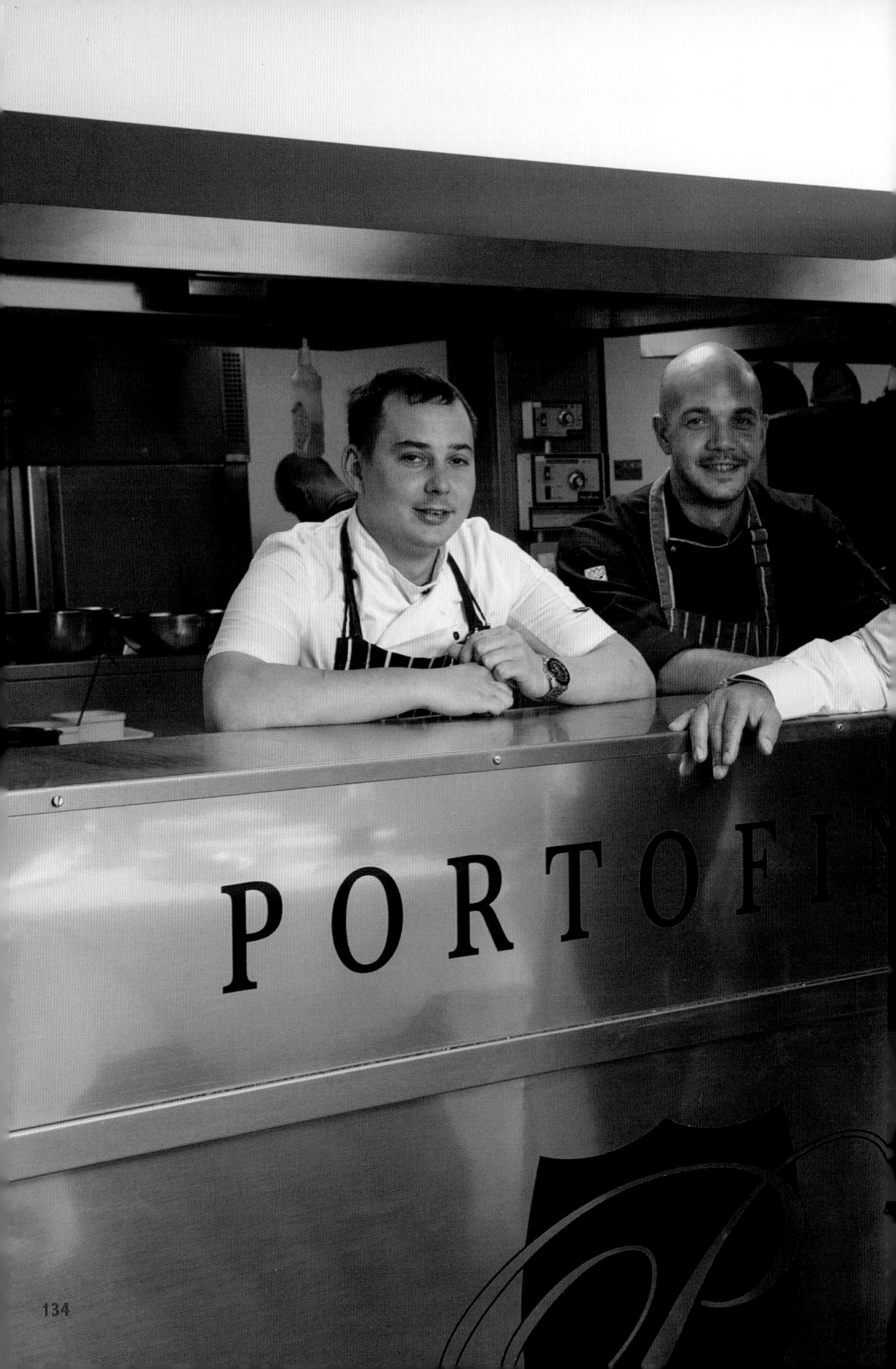
PORTOFIN

MANX WHITE CRAB MEAT, LOBSTER, SMOKED SALMON AND PARSLEY SOUFFLÉ WITH GRILLED ASPARAGUS AND TOMATO CHUTNEY

SERVES 4

Ingredients

Chutney

250g red onions (diced)
500g fresh tomatoes (chopped)
2 red chillies (deseeded and sliced)
75ml red wine vinegar
140g brown sugar

Soufflé

1 x 226g cooked lobster
150g white crab meat (picked through and seasoned)
150g smoked salmon (diced)
1 bunch of parsley (chopped)
50g Manx butter
50g Laxey Mill flour
150ml milk
4 egg whites

To Serve

1 bunch of asparagus (blanched and refreshed)
dressed salad

4 ramekins lined with butter and grated Parmesan cheese

Method

For the Chutney

Sweat the onions, tomatoes and chillies in a saucepan.
Add the vinegar and sugar then simmer for 20 minutes and set aside for later.

For the Soufflé

Preheat oven to 180°C/gas 4
Butter 4 ramekins and dust with finely grated Parmesan. Set aside.
Blanch the lobster for 2 minutes, cool then remove the meat and cut into chunks.
Place the lobster, crab meat, smoked salmon and parsley in a bowl, mix well and season to taste.
Melt the butter in a thick-bottomed saucepan then add the flour, stirring constantly. Allow to cook out for 2 minutes, then gradually add the milk and cook out for further 2 minutes.
Pour the sauce into a mixing bowl, stir the crab, lobster and salmon mix into the sauce then set aside.
Next, in a separate bowl, whisk the egg whites to form stiff peaks then gently fold into the lobster mix.
Divide into ramekins and bake in a bain-marie in the preheated oven for approx. 13 minutes.

To Serve

About 1 minute before serving, grill the blanched and refreshed asparagus and transfer to each plate along with the soufflé. Finish with the chutney and a dressed salad.

FILLET OF MANX BEEF AND GREEBA MUSHROOM GRATIN WITH GARLIC PURÉE

SERVES 4

Ingredients

904g prime Manx fillet beef (rolled in cling film and refrigerated)

Garlic Purée
150g wild Manx garlic leaves
150g fresh spinach
500ml boiling water
30g butter
salt and pepper

Gratin
250g Greeba mushrooms
2 tbsp Dijon mustard
100g Parmesan cheese (grated)
salt and pepper

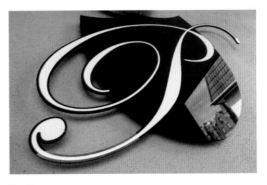

To Serve
reduced red wine sauce

Method

For the Purée
In a saucepan sweat down the garlic and spinach leaves, then add the water and leave for 2 minutes. Drain the leaves and place in a blender, gradually adding a little water to create the consistency you prefer. Put the blended leaves through a fine chinois or sieve, then transfer to the saucepan. Heat gently, add the butter and season to taste. Set aside.

For the Gratin
Preheat oven to 200°C/gas 6
Dice the mushrooms and sweat down in a saucepan until cooked. Drain the mushrooms then add the mustard and cheese. Mix well and season with salt and pepper.
Cut the fillet into 4 x 226g steaks. Seal them off in a hot pan then place on a baking tray. Take the mushroom gratin mix and place on top of the fillets. Bake in the oven at 200°C for 7 minutes.

To Serve
Place the purée on the plate and arrange the steak on top, finish with a reduced red wine sauce.

STRAWBERRY CUSTARD TART WITH RHUBARB JAM AND VANILLA ICE CREAM

SERVES 4

Ingredients

Rhubarb Jam
900g rhubarb
113g sugar
½ tbsp cinnamon

Sweet Pastry
125g soft butter
90g caster sugar
1 whole egg
1 vanilla pod
250g plain flour

Egg Custard Mix
10 egg yolks
3 whole eggs
300ml milk
400ml double cream
75g caster sugar
nutmeg (grated)

To Serve
strawberries
strawberry jelly to glaze
vanilla ice cream

Method

For the Rhubarb Jam
Dice the rhubarb and cook slowly in a saucepan with the sugar. Once the sugar has dissolved add the cinnamon and continue to cook, whilst stirring, until the mixture forms a jam consistency. Set aside.

For the Sweet Pastry
Preheat oven to 160°C/gas 3

Beat the butter, sugar and egg together until pale and creamy. Halve the vanilla pod and scrape away the seeds, then add the vanilla seeds and flour to the mixture. Mix together until a firm dough is formed.
Roll the pastry into a ball and leave to set in the fridge. Once chilled, roll out the pastry and place in a suitable pastry case. Blind bake at 160°C for 20 minutes.

For the Egg Custard Mix
Preheat oven to 130°C/gas 1
Lightly whisk the eggs yolks and whole eggs in a large bowl.
Warm the milk, cream and sugar in a saucepan, then gradually pour over the eggs, whisking continuously. Strain and skim the mixture, then pour into the blind baked pastry case. Grate fresh nutmeg on top and bake at 130°C for 1 hour and leave to cool.

To Serve
When cooled slice the strawberries and arrange over the top of the tart until covered and glaze with strawberry jelly. Serve with a spoon of the rhubarb jam and vanilla ice cream.

L'EXPERIENCE

Summerhill, Isle of Man IM2 4PL
01624 623103
www.lex.co.im

*B*onjour mes amis, if you look closely at the bottom of Summerhill Road you will notice a little slice of France. Nestled between the red and blue tablecloths are the owners of this establishment – Michael runs the kitchen and Belinda is the Front of House. Married couple Michael and Belinda met at catering college, both their fathers were chefs and owning a restaurant was their dream from the beginning. After catering college Michael served in the Royal Green Jackets in the British army and Belinda worked in various catering roles within schools and restaurants. L'Experience meant a great deal to Michael and Belinda as Michael had worked there as a boy. They bought L'Experience in 2009 and have never looked back; they boast the best French onion soup this side of the channel.

Away from the hustle and bustle of town, L'Experience host many events in the restaurant. They arrange themed evenings such as 'Allo Allo' and support charities by having special fundraising evenings. They also work with the schools on the Island and do French tasting classes: the owners feel that teaching children about cooking is a valuable life skill.

As cooking is such a tremendous part of Michael and Belinda's lives, everything at L'Experience is cooked to order and the staff pride themselves on being as hospitable as possible and will bend to anyone's needs or preferences. So come and visit the heart of France in the Isle of Man, you will never want to go back!

Au Revoir, à bientôt!

Manx queenies on local Pork F...
10

Douglas Bay Mackerel on Potato
7

Whole Port st mary lobster with
Butter & ... nuggets
26

East co... ...ock with ...em
17

Conish ... with war...
19

144

FRENCH ONION SOUP

SERVES 4

Ingredients

50g Manx butter
1 tbsp olive oil
1kg onions (halved and thinly sliced)
1 tsp sugar
4 garlic cloves (thinly sliced)
2 tbsp plain Laxey flour
250ml dry white wine
1.3 ltr hot strongly-flavoured beef stock

To Serve

4–8 thin slices French bread (depending on size, toasted)
400g Manx mild red Cheddar (grated)
100g Gruyère cheese (finely grated)

Method

Melt the butter with the oil in a large heavy-based saucepan. Add the onions and fry with the lid on for 10 minutes until soft. Sprinkle in the sugar and cook for 20 minutes more, stirring frequently, until caramelised. The onions should be really golden, full of flavour and soft when pinched between your fingers. Take care towards the end to ensure that they don't burn.

Add the garlic for the final few minutes of the onions' cooking time, then sprinkle in the flour and stir well. Increase the heat and keep stirring as you gradually add the wine, followed by the hot stock. Cover and simmer for 15–20 minutes.

To Serve

Turn on the grill. Ladle the soup into heatproof bowls. Put a slice or two of toasted French bread on top of the bowls of soup, pile on the Cheddar cheese and top with Gruyère. Grill until melted and crispy.

TOURNEDOS ROSSINI

SERVES 4

Ingredients

Rossini
4 x 200g beef fillet steak (from Harrison and Garrett)
200g pâté
4 rashers of streaky bacon
1 tbsp olive oil
25g Manx butter

Sauce
250ml red wine
200ml beef stock
5 peppercorns
50g unsalted Manx butter

Method

For the Rossini
Cut a hole in the side of the fillet steaks then pipe the pâté into the middle. Wrap the bacon around the meat and use a cocktail stick to hold the bacon securely onto the steak, covering the hole where the pâté is.
Heat a frying pan and add the oil and butter. Cook the steaks to your liking, remove from the pan and place aside to rest.

For the Sauce
Add the red wine to the pan you cooked the steaks in, heat gently and deglaze the pan by scraping off the stuck on crispy bits left over from cooking the steak. Cook until the volume of liquid is reduced by half, then add the beef stock and peppercorns. Cook for 2–3 minutes, then strain through a fine sieve into a clean pan and finish with a knob of butter.

To Serve
Plate up the steaks, and pour over the sauce.

ORANGE GRAND MARNIER

SERVES 4

Ingredients

6 oranges
2 cinnamon sticks
337g sugar
80ml water
30ml Grand Marnier

To Serve
whipped cream or ice cream

Method

Cut the rind and any white pith from 5 of the oranges, then slice into thin rounds. Place in a colander, allowing the juices to drain into a bowl. Squeeze the juice from the extra orange and add to the reserved juice. Arrange the oranges in a serving dish with the cinnamon sticks.

Combine the sugar and water in a tall saucepan and stir until the sugar has dissolved. Heat until the sugar turns a deep golden colour (this will take about 10 minutes on a medium-high heat). Combine the reserved orange juice and the Grand Marnier.

Turn off the heat, stand back and pour in the combined orange juice and Grand Marnier. Because of the difference in temperature the caramel will sputter but this will soon subside.

Stir until the syrup is smooth, then pour over the oranges, cover with plastic wrap and place in the refrigerator for several hours or overnight to marinate.

To Serve
Serve chilled, as is, or with whipped cream or ice cream.

MILNTOWN

Milntown, Lezayre, Isle of Man, IM7 2AB
01624 818091
www.milntown.org

With its own kitchen garden just a stone's throw from where the food is prepared, Milntown Café chef Sonia Deakin has no difficulty offering a menu packed with fresh, seasonal ingredients.

The emphasis on using local produce is part of the ethos of Milntown, a popular family-friendly visitor attraction which was the home of the powerful Christian family for more than 500 years.

It was latterly owned by Sir Clive Edwards, whose family were wealthy Welsh foundry-owners. He loved the Isle of Man and bequeathed the estate in trust for the benefit of the Manx people.

At the heart of the Milntown estate, surrounded by 15 acres of mature woodland, is a splendid white mansion, whose crenulated walls look magnificent etched against a clear blue sky. House tours are held throughout the season.

Close to the house are a flourishing flower garden and a sunny and secluded walled garden, where fruit, vegetables and herbs are grown especially for the table.

Milntown Café is set in a light and spacious conservatory with wonderful views of the walled garden. The conservatory is a recent addition that perfectly harmonises with the main house. It is an ideal place for morning coffee, a hearty lunch after a garden visit, or a relaxing afternoon tea.

The menu offers a wide selection of home-cooked seasonal dishes, cakes and desserts. There is also a children's menu.

The bread is home-baked, as are the cakes and puddings, which often utilise fruit such as apples and rhubarb from the garden.

Catering manager Louise Bignall said: 'Our customers are looking for good tasty food and friendly service in a relaxed setting. Many come in for lunch after visiting the gardens and they will come back in again for tea and cake before leaving'.

The garden team work closely with the chef who decides on the day's menu. The specials' board is dictated by what is seasonally available and always features leafy salads based on what can be plucked fresh from the garden, which is run using organic methods.

The three courses featured here include peas, mint, fennel and raspberries – all fresh from the garden of course – but easily replicated at home.

For up-to-the-minute information on opening hours and house tours visit the website: www.milntown.org or telephone 01624 818091.

GARDEN PEA, MINT AND CRÈME FRAICHE SOUP

SERVES 4

Ingredients

250g garden peas
4 tbsp fresh mint
850ml vegetable stock
2 tbsp crème fraiche
pinch of caster sugar
salt and pepper

Method

Put the fresh peas, fresh mint, vegetable stock and caster sugar into a saucepan. Bring to the boil and then simmer for 10 minutes.

Remove from the heat and blend all the ingredients together in a food processor or by using a hand blender. Add the crème fraiche and blend again. Season to taste and serve with delicious home made Milntown bread.

KING PRAWN AND FENNEL RISOTTO
SERVES 4

Ingredients

1.2 ltr vegetable stock
1 tbsp olive oil
1 onion (chopped)
1 clove garlic (chopped)
1 small bulb Milntown fennel (finely chopped)
300g risotto rice
300g raw king prawns
1 lemon (zest and juice)
100ml double cream
salt and pepper

Method

Pour the vegetable stock into a saucepan, bring to the boil and simmer.

In a large saucepan heat the oil, add the onion, garlic and Milntown fennel and cook on a low heat for 10 minutes. Add the rice and stir for a couple of minutes until hot, increase the heat to medium and slowly add the stock a ladle at a time, stirring constantly, making sure the stock is absorbed into the rice before adding the next ladleful. When the rice is almost cooked add the king prawns, lemon zest and seasoning, continue cooking for 4 minutes until the prawns have turned pink.

Remove from the heat and stir in the lemon juice and double cream, season to taste and allow to rest for 2 minutes before serving.

DARK CHOCOLATE AND RASPBERRY TART

SERVES 4

Ingredients

400g butter biscuits
200g butter (melted) plus extra for greasing
2 tbsp honey
400g dark chocolate
400ml double cream
2 tsp vanilla extract
4 tbsp icing sugar
150g fresh raspberries

Method

Grease a 10" loose-bottomed flan tin with melted butter. Put the biscuits in a food processor and blitz until they have the consistency of breadcrumbs, tip into a bowl and add the melted butter and honey, then tip into the flan case. Press the mixture firmly into the tin and put into the fridge for 20 minutes.

Place the dark chocolate into a bowl over a pan of simmering water (making sure that the bowl does not touch the water) and allow to melt.

In another bowl whisk the double cream, vanilla and icing sugar together until it forms quite stiff peaks.

When the chocolate has melted, remove from the heat and allow to cool for a couple of minutes.

Remove the base from the fridge and sprinkle the fresh raspberries over the base.

Fold the melted chocolate into the cream mixture and pour over the base, then place in the fridge to set for a minimum of 2 hours.

Cut and serve as desired.

The Island Kitchen : Milntown

CAFÉ ROSA RESTAURANT

Glen Duff, Lezayre, Ramsey, Isle of Man IM7 2AT
01624 816609
www.caferosa.org

Café Rosa Restaurant is an elegant little establishment nestled in a quaint countryside garden setting just outside of Ramsey. With an eclectic interior of antiques, paintings and traditionally dressed tables and seating, it offers a warm, casual atmosphere in which to unwind and savour varied cuisine.

Café Rosa is renowned for its signature two-course set-price lunch menu (including tea or coffee) offering an uncommonly wide choice of mains, with everything from grilled fish and vibrant salads right through to Ballavair Manx Sirloin. The hand-peeled rustic chips, using potatoes sourced from St. Judes village, remain ever popular.

Undoubtedly the main attraction, however, is the Island's largest choice of 100% homemade desserts, each created by Rosa on-site using Laxey Glen Mill flour and local free-range eggs. Every dessert is beautifully presented with patterned sauce garnishes, chocolate tuiles and accompanied with Manx ice cream and cream.

Diners choose from an ample photographic dessert menu consisting of decadent creations such as feather-light pear and almond sponge, triple-layer fruit gateau, deep-base lemon meringue pie, crème caramels, and several fruit meringue towers.

Every Sunday the finest Manx lamb, beef, pork and a host of lighter and vegetarian options are offered alongside the prerequisite roast potatoes, Yorkshire puddings, stuffing and trimmings – making it a preferred destination for whiling away leisurely weekends amongst friends and family.

Proprietors Chef Bob and Rosa Phillips are amongst the Island's longest-serving restaurateurs, cooking and serving continuously since 1982 when they opened their first restaurant, the eponymous La Rosette Restaurant in the south of the Island, in Ballasalla village. This fine dining restaurant won UK acclaim, including listing in the Egon Ronay and Michelin Guides, receiving the prestigious Prix Armagnac Janneau for French cuisine.

Prior to moving to the Island, the couple met whilst working in various top London hotels on Park Lane, as both chef and front of house respectively. Chef Bob has also cooked for the royal family whilst a retained chef at Lancaster House, a St. James mansion owned by HM government.

In 1995, the couple closed La Rosette and opened Café Rosa in the beautiful Manx countryside and whilst the fayre may be simpler these days, the same high standards and dedication to attentive service remain.

Diners can rest assured a warm welcome awaits in this delightful outpost of the Island's dining scene, a veritable magnet for the dessert fan.

ORGANIC WATERCRESS AND POTATO SOUP
SERVES 4

Use locally-grown ingredients wherever possible
This soup does not contain any oil or butter,
making for a lighter option. The soup's thickness
is derived from using starchy white Manx
potatoes.

Ingredients

100g organic watercress (finely chopped)
400g starchy Manx potatoes (diced)
100g white onion (diced)
1 tsp chicken stock cube (crumbled) or 28g pre-prepared
'stock pot'
¼ tsp cracked black pepper
750ml boiling water

To Serve
a sprinkle of croutons
sprig of watercress

Method

Place all the prepared ingredients into a soup maker (or
alternatively a large saucepan) and cover with boiling
water.
Place the lid on the soup maker – select 'smooth' mode
and wait 21 minutes, everything is automatic and takes
the hard work out of making this delicious starter.
More traditionally, place all the ingredients in a large
saucepan, bring to the boil, simmer for 21 minutes and
place into a liquidiser or food processor, or pass through
a wire sieve with the back of a ladle.

To Serve
Serve with a sprig of watercress and a sprinkling of
simple croutons.

The Island Kitchen : Cafe Rosa

BAKED DOVER SOLE WITH PRAWNS IN A WHITE WINE, BUTTER AND LEMON VELOUTÉ

SERVES 4

Use locally landed seafood wherever possible
This dish goes nicely with a variety of steamed
vegetables (widely available from farmers'
markets – these will always taste better) or a
leafy salad dressed with local Ellerslie Farm
rapeseed oil.

Ingredients

1 Dover sole (approx. 700–800g)
300g creel-caught prawns (peeled)
100g Isle of Man Creamery butter
300ml medium white wine
2 tsp fresh lemon juice
zest of 1 lemon (grated)
1 tsp corn starch
turmeric (optional)
salt and pepper

To Serve
pinch of chopped parsley/chives (optional)

Method

Preheat oven to 200°C/gas 6
When buying Dover sole, ask your fishmonger to skin
both sides of the fish (and remove the head), filleting and
folding back the centre, to allow room for the prawns.
Season the sole with salt and pepper, with perhaps a
sprinkle of turmeric for colour.
Fill the centre with the prawns, placing the fish onto a
sheet of lightly oiled parchment paper.
Place the fish on a baking tray and cook in a preheated
oven at 200°C for approximately 15–20 minutes (or until
golden brown).
For the sauce, simply combine the butter, white wine and

lemon juice/zest in a small pan, bring to the boil, then
simmer whilst slowly stirring in the corn starch (which
should be been diluted with 2 tbsp of water in a cup)
until the sauce has lightly thickened.
Pour all over the fish and serve. Top with a sprinkle of
chopped parsley/chives (optional).

LEMON MERINGUE PIE

SERVES 4

Ingredients

Sweet Pastry Case
185g Isle of Man Creamery butter
500g Laxey Glen Mills white flour
125g caster sugar
2 large free-range eggs
60ml water
2 drops vanilla essence

Lemon Curd Filling
6 large lemons (juice and zest, grated)
8 free-range egg yolks
250g caster sugar
125g Isle of Man Creamery butter
300ml water
4 drops of yellow food colouring
90g corn starch

Meringue Topping
8 large free-range egg whites
750g caster sugar

Method

For the Sweet Pastry Case
Preheat oven to 200°C / gas 6
Rub the butter into the flour until a sandy texture is obtained.
Mix the sugar, eggs, water and vanilla essence in a jug, then fold into the butter and flour. Gently knead together to form a paste and place into a fridge to cool for 30 minutes.
Roll out the paste on a floured surface, approx. 3–4mm thick. Line a pre-greased suitable cake ring, or tin, with the paste, pricking the bottom with a fork.
Cook in the preheated oven at 200°C for approx. 10–15 minutes until lightly browned.

For the Lemon Curd Filling
Place the lemon zest and juice, egg yolk (no whites), caster sugar, butter, water and yellow colouring into a thick-bottomed saucepan. Weigh out 90g of corn starch and dilute with 3 tablespoons of water in a cup, keeping to one side ready for use.
Place the pan on the heat, gently bringing up to a simmer whilst slowly adding and stirring in the corn starch until the curd has thickened.
Immediately pour the mixture into the sweet pastry case, and leave to cool.

For the Meringue Topping
Preheat oven to 100°C/gas ¼
Pour the egg whites into an electric food processor with a whisk attachment. Whisk on the top speed until the whites are thick and fluffy.
Gently fold in the caster sugar, and either pipe or spoon on top of the cooled lemon curd.
Place in a preheated oven at 100°C for approximately 10–15 minutes until lightly browned.
Cool and refrigerate to allow for easier slicing.

RAMSEY
AND THE NORTH

JEAN-PIERRE'S BISTRO

Jean-Pierre's Bistro, Court Row, Ramsey, IM8 1JS
01624 819839
www.jeanpierresbistro.com

Growing up amongst the herbs, spices and home-grown vegetables of his Italian grandmother's little kitchen, Jean-Pierre loved to stir sauces, pick courgette flowers and roll fresh pasta. He was destined to be a chef. Jean-Pierre qualified in Nice, France and worked at La Columbe D'Or in St Paul De Vence, where the demands of discerning diners, especially for fresh Mediterranean seafood, encouraged his special flair with fish. After being a Chef De Partie at La Grande Albion in Cannes, he ventured out to experience the cuisine of French Polynesia and worked as a Sous Chef in Tahiti and the Cook Islands. Again, he specialised in seafood and fresh fish and now has a passion for choosing the finest fish for the Bistro's Specials. When he returned to France, Jean-Pierre took his culinary talent to Courchevel in the French Alps where he worked at a top hotel. Our chef continued refining his skills on the sun-drenched beaches of St Tropez, working at both the resort as well as doing private dining parties at prestigious homes.

At the other end of the world, in sunny South Africa, an entrepreneur, businessman and excellent trout farmer, Gary Charsley and his wife, Carol, brought up a little girl, Kerry, to be adventurous, with a desire to explore the world. Kerry's ambitions led her to France, where the two hemispheres met on the ski slopes of Courchevel and from here a perfect future came to life. They were married in France, and then moved to Cornwall where Jean-Pierre became the Head Pastry Chef at

The Headland Hotel, followed by attaining the accolade of Executive Chef at Sands Resort in Porth, Cornwall. Here he was able to master the produce, menu favourites and tastes of the British diners.

Meanwhile, Gary and Carol Charsley left South Africa to settle on the beautiful gem of the Isle of Man, in the North Irish Sea. The Island provides such a perfect environment for families to grow and develop, that Jean-Pierre moved his family to be closer to the larger family and open a restaurant together. The family had a vision to create a venue and food that would enhance the dining experience for Manx diners. After looking around the Island they chose Ramsey, and took on the challenge of turning the Old Post Office into a kitchen and dining room that would meet their shared vision.

The restaurant consistently provides a high quality dining experience, using fresh Manx produce, naturally cooked with a French flavour. The atmosphere is warm and inviting and the food is absolutely exquisite. The restaurant is fully licensed too. The four adult members of the family are all actively involved in the business, each performing a different but complementary role to ensure success. We are very proud to run a family-owned and managed business which meets the needs of the Island's dining community. Having also recently opened a delicatessen at Jean-Pierre's the family has cemented their reputation for excellent produce, flavoursome food and brilliant service.

GREEBA MUSHROOM AND PARMA HAM HOMEMADE RAVIOLI, SAGE VELOUTÉ AND TRUFFLE OIL

SERVES 4

Ingredients

Ravioli Filling
7g butter
7g plain flour
50ml milk
4 medium-sized closed-cup mushrooms
2 slices Parma ham
1 garlic clove (finely chopped)
20g parsley (finely chopped)
a pinch of nutmeg
salt and pepper

Ravioli Dough
280g strong white flour
2 whole eggs
2 egg yolks
1 tbsp olive oil
1 egg (beaten with a little water)

Sage Velouté
10g butter (plus 7g to thicken sauce)
1 shallot (finely chopped)
100ml white wine
100ml vegetable stock
100ml cream
7g plain flour
4 fresh sage leaves (finely chopped)

To Serve
rocket leaves
Parmesan cheese shavings
truffle oil

Method

For the Ravioli Filling
Make a béchamel sauce: melt the butter in a medium saucepan and add the flour when the butter is starting to bubble. Whisk until combined and then add the milk. Keep stirring until bubbly and thick. Add salt and pepper and a pinch of ground nutmeg.
Place on the side and reserve for later.
Slice the mushrooms finely and pan-fry in a little butter until tender. Add the chopped Parma ham, chopped garlic and chopped parsley. Fold the mushroom mix into the béchamel sauce and reserve again.

For the Ravioli Dough
Heap the flour into a mound with a well in the centre. Place the eggs, egg yolk and oil into the well, whisk gently with a fork and slowly start dragging the flour into the egg mixture. Knead by hand until all the ingredients are well combined and the dough is smooth and elastic (about 10 minutes).
Wrap the dough in cling film and let it rest at room temperature for 30 minutes.

For the Sage Velouté
While the ravioli dough is resting, make the sauce:
Melt 10g of butter in a saucepan with the chopped shallot and cook for a minute or two until the shallot loses its colour. Add the white wine and reduce by a third. Add the vegetable stock and reduce again by half. Add the cream and cook for 15 minutes.
In a separate pan heat 7g of butter until bubbly and add the 7g of flour. Mix thoroughly, then use this mixture to thicken the sauce, whisking constantly.
Season to taste and add the sage.

To Finish

Cut a piece of dough roughly the size of an egg. Using a pasta machine, roll the dough into sheets ⅛ inch thick. Spoon the filling on 1 pasta sheet, leaving 1 inch between each mound of filling. Using a pastry brush, lightly wet the pasta around the filling with the egg beaten in water. Cover with a second pastry sheet, press together to seal the edges around the filling and press out any excess air.

Cut individual ravioli with a knife.

To Serve

Bring a large pot of lightly salted water to the boil. Add the ravioli all at once and gently stir to submerge. Cook uncovered for 2–3 minutes.

Drain the ravioli thoroughly, serve with the sauce on top and decorate with rocket leaves, Parmesan shavings and some truffle oil.

ROAST MANX PORK TENDERLOIN FILLED WITH APPLE STUFFING AND DRIZZLED WITH CIDER CREAM SAUCE, SERVED WITH RUNNER BEANS À LA FRANÇAISE

SERVES 4

Ingredients

Pork Tenderloin

4 x 150g of Manx pork tenderloin
20g Isle of Man Creamery butter (with extra for frying)
20g Manx onion (finely diced)
1 tsp garlic (finely chopped)
100g Manx apples (diced)
50ml Discovery Manx apple juice
250ml Manx dry cider
200g Manx sausage meat
4 sage leaves (chopped)
4 pinches of breadcrumbs
8 slices Manx streaky bacon
salt and pepper
a piece of kitchen string for tying

Creamy Sauce

10g Isle of Man Creamery butter
20g Manx onions (diced)
100ml Manx dry apple cider
100ml Discovery Manx apple juice
200ml beef stock
400ml Isle of Man Creamery double cream

Runner Beans

200g Manx runner beans
10g Isle of Man Creamery butter
20g Manx onion (diced)
½ tsp garlic (chopped)
2 slices Manx streaky bacon
2 Manx lettuce leaves (sliced)

To Serve

4 Manx mustard salad leaves
Potato Maxime: cut potato thinly and layer in a circle. Brush with melted butter and crisp in the oven for 5 minutes before being ready to serve.

Method

For the Pork

Preheat oven to 220°C/gas 7
Trim the pork tenderloin, then using a sharp knife make a lengthwise cut down the centre of the meat, cutting to, but not through, the other side.
Spread the meat flat and pound lightly but finely. Set aside for later..
In a pan, melt the butter over a medium heat and add onions and garlic. Cook for approx. 1 minute before adding the apples and deglaze with the apple juice and apple cider.
Turn the heat down and reduce until a third of the liquid remains (whilst waiting for it to reduce, put a pot of water on to bring to the boil – use this later for the runner beans).
Next add the sausage meat, sage, and breadcrumbs to the reduced mixture and season with salt and pepper to taste. Mix well.
Season the tenderloin, spoon the stuffing evenly over the meat, then roll the tenderloin up (jelly roll style) and secure with the slices of streaky bacon around the outside. Tie the meat with string at regular intervals (approx. 1 inch).

Pan-fry the tenderloin in butter on both sides, sprinkle with pepper and roast uncovered in a 220°C oven for approx. 20 minutes or until the meat is tender and the juices run clear.

Transfer to a warm platter, remove the strings and keep warm.

For the Sauce

Whilst pork is in the oven prepare the sauce:
Melt the butter in a saucepan, add the onions and cook for 1 minute before deglazing with cider and apple juice. Reduce until a third of the liquid remains. Add the beef stock and again allow to reduce until half of the liquid remains. Add the cream and cook for 10 minutes until thickened. Season to taste.

For the Runner Beans

Whilst the sauce is thickening prepare the runner beans:
Cook the runner beans in salted boiling water until al dente, then cool down in iced water to stop them cooking and to keep the nice fresh green colour. Slice finely on the diagonal.

Melt the butter in a pan then add the diced onions and garlic, and cook for 1 minute. Add the chopped streaky bacon and cook for a further 1 minute. Add the sliced runner beans and sliced lettuce leaves and toss for 30 seconds. Remove from the heat and keep warm.

To Serve

On a warm plate, position the runner beans in the centre, gently placing the pork tenderloin in 4 pieces around the beans. Spoon the sauce over and around the edge. Decorate with Potato Maxime and mustard salad leaves.

CHOCOLATE AND ORANGE MARQUIS WITH VANILLA CRÈME ANGLAISE AND CANDIED ORANGE ZEST

SERVES 4

Ingredients

Marquis
100g good quality dark chocolate
50g butter
1 tbsp cocoa powder
6 egg yolks
1 orange (grated zest)
125ml double cream
50g caster sugar

Crème Anglaise
3 egg yolks
60g caster sugar
250ml milk
2 tsp vanilla extract

To Serve
1 orange (finely sliced zest)
100ml water
100ml caster sugar

Method

For the Marquis
Melt the chocolate and butter in a glass bowl on top of a pan of boiling water, making sure the water does not touch the bowl.
Add the cocoa powder, mix and reserve.
When the preparation is lukewarm, mix in the egg yolks and grated orange zest.
In another bowl whip the double cream with the caster sugar to form soft peaks then, with a spatula, add to the chocolate preparation.
Put in a rectangular mould and set in the fridge for 4 hours.

For the Crème Anglaise
Whisk the egg yolks and sugar together until smooth.
Heat the milk and vanilla extract in a saucepan until boiling, then slowly pour the hot milk mixture into the egg yolk, mixing constantly.
Transfer back to the pan and cook the mixture, stirring constantly, on a low heat until it thickens, but do not allow to boil!

To Serve
Finely slice the zest of an orange and boil in a syrup made with 100ml water and 100ml caster sugar until the zest is translucent and the syrup is reduced.
Slice the Marquis, place on a plate with a dollop of the crème anglaise and top with the candied orange zest.

PEEL

FILBEY'S

Peel Harbour, Peel, Isle of Man, IM5 1AR
01624 844144
www.filbeys.com

It has been a lifelong dream for us to open our own little restaurant on the Isle of Man and with a lot of hard work we have finally got there. To be located in Peel with the harbour and castle views really makes it special. The Isle of Man gives us fantastic local produce on our doorstep and every year it just keeps getting better; to have all these fresh ingredients to work with every day is a chef's dream. Also, to quench your thirst, the Island makes its very own ales, lagers, ciders, mineral waters and fruit juices. I hope you enjoy some simple recipes below that you can try at home and that one day you can enjoy an experience here on the Isle of Man.

MANX KING SCALLOPS

SERVES 4

Ingredients

1 small black pudding log (sliced into 12 x 1cm slices)
4 slices of locally smoked Manx bacon
12 Manx king scallops (roe removed)
4 wedges of lemon
rock salt

To Serve

Cauliflower purée and micro herbs for decoration

Method

Set the grill on medium and place the black pudding and smoked bacon in a tray under the grill for 5 minutes. Place your scallops on a plate and season with a little sprinkle of rock salt, then get a frying pan on with a splash of oil nice and hot. After the 5 minutes is up flip the black pudding and shake the bacon, then drop the scallops into the pan and cook on each side for 1½ minutes. Turn the heat off then squeeze some lemon juice on them.

To Serve

Quickly divide your cauliflower purée onto individual plates and place 3 slices of black pudding on the purée, top each piece with a king scallop and place the smoked bacon on top. Serve with a wedge of lemon and finish with micro herbs for decoration.

HAKE STEAK TOPPED WITH LOBSTER PÂTÉ AND HALF A LOBSTER TAIL

SERVES 4

Ingredients

4 x 145–170g hake fillet steaks
1 lemon
3 garlic cloves
small bunch of fresh herbs
small glass of wine
16 boiled potatoes (sliced)
2 courgettes (sliced)
2 cooked lobsters
butter
salt and pepper

Lobster Pâté

4 lobster claws
3 tbsp cream cheese
small bunch of fresh herbs (chopped)
1 lemon (zest and juice)
1 lime (zest and juice)

To Serve

edible flowers
fresh herbs

Method

Preheat oven to 200°C/gas 6
Prepare a pan of boiling water to cook the lobster.
Take a piece of tinfoil 40cm x 40cm and fold in half, place the hake fillets on one half and season, slice the lemon in half and squeeze half over the fish. Fold the 2 smaller sides tightly so you are left with one opening, throw in the garlic, fresh herbs and wine and seal the parcel tight. Place it in the oven for 14–16 minutes, when it's puffed up its ready! Place the sliced potato and courgettes in a tray with seasoning and cook for the final 10 minutes

before serving.
Place the lobsters in the pan for 10 minutes then run under cold water, remove the tails and half them. Top with butter and lemon juice and set aside on a tray for later.

For the Pâté

Remove the meat from the lobster claws and place in a bowl with the cream cheese and herbs. Zest the lemon and lime before juicing, then add the zest and juice into the lobster mixture, mix well and keep to one side.

To Serve

Turn on your grill. When your foil is puffed up, and the hake is ready, carefully slice the top piece of foil off and top the steaks with pâté and half a lobster tail then place under the lowest part of the grill for a few minutes. Place your potatoes and courgettes in the centre of a serving plate with the hake on top, pour some of the cooking juices around the outside and finish with edible flowers or fresh herbs.

The Island Kitchen : Filbey's

BASIL INFUSED PANNA COTTA WITH SUMMER BERRIES
SERVES 4

Ingredients

4 sheets of leaf gelatine
250ml Manx full-fat milk
250ml Manx double cream
1 vanilla pod
a handful of fresh basil
a good squeeze of Manx honey
a small handful of mixed berries (raspberries, strawberries, redcurrants, blueberries etc.)

To Serve
mint leaves
sugar basket (optional)

Method

Place the gelatine sheets in cold water to soak.
Put the milk and cream in a pan and bring to a simmer.

Halve the vanilla pod and remove the seeds then add all to the pan. Next add the basil and allow to infuse for 5 minutes before adding the honey. Remove the gelatine from the water, squeeze off the excess water, add to the pan and stir until dissolved. Remove the pan from the heat and cool for a minute, then pour the pan contents through a sieve to remove the basil and vanilla pod. Divide the mixture between 4 ramekins or moulds and chill for 2 hours.

To Serve
When you are ready to serve prepare a small bowl of hot water, deep enough to sit the moulds/ramekins in, place them in the water for 10 seconds. Remove from the water, turn upside down onto a plate and carefully release. Place the mixed berries on top of the panna cotta or around the plate. In the restaurant we finish the dish with a few mint leaves and sugar basket. Enjoy!

The Island Kitchen : Filbey's

PEEL

THE BOATYARD

The Boatyard Restaurant, Mariners Wharf, East Quay, Peel, Isle of Man IM5 1AR
01624 845470
www.theboatyardpeel.com

The Mowat family opened The Boatyard Restaurant in May 2013 just after one of the worst winters the Island had experienced in over 30 years, with the west side of the Island effectively severed from the east by heavy snowfalls. Situated in the beautiful seaside town of Peel, on the Island's west coast, the restaurant enjoys a prominent location on the town's historic East Quay with superb views overlooking the marina and traditional fishing harbour. Known locally as Sunset City, visitors to Peel are awarded some of the Island's most sensational sunsets – weather permitting. Peel also boasts two beautiful beaches as well as a working harbour, ancient castle and historic town making it a popular attraction for families, day trippers, and couples.

Built on the site of a former shipbuilding yard, the restaurant's name 'The Boatyard' became an obvious choice as a way of maintaining a connection to the building's past and town's seafaring heritage. Continuing the coastal and seaside theme into the restaurant, the interior has been tastefully designed to bring out the playful side of this Manx seaside town with shades of blue, maritime décor and shipping flags. During the day, the restaurant is a popular location for the many visitors, families and friends enjoying the rugged coastal paths, sandy beaches and winding lanes Peel have to offer. The mood changes as the evening draws in and the candlelit dining room creates a warm and welcoming atmosphere.

The Boatyard's menu reflects its coastal location and has been developed around our philosophy of using as many local ingredients and as much local produce as possible. Through an opening into the kitchen, Head Chef Stephen Kelly and his team prepare dishes made fresh to order, adding to the overall theatre of dining at The Boatyard. Fresh local fish and seafood, much of which is sourced from boats arriving just a few hundred feet from the restaurant, features prominently across our menus with a variety of daily blackboard specials highlighting the catch of the day. Sourcing local produce has been made a lot easier in the past few years as the Island has seen a growth in independent food and drink producers, many of which are now regular suppliers to our restaurant, including Staarvey Farm salad leaves and herbs, Greeba Farm mushrooms, Peel smoked kippers and Manx lobsters from Niarbyl to highlight just a few within a few miles of the restaurant. Our drinks menu also features many locally crafted beverages including artisan beers from the Hooded Ram Brewery, Manx fruit juices and sparkling pressés from the Apple Orphanage, and Manx mineral water from the Green Mann situated just down the road in St Johns.

DEEP-FRIED SQUID IN A POLENTA, CHILLI AND FENNEL COATING WITH CRÈME FRAICHE AND CHILLI JAM

SERVES 4

Ingredients

4 medium-sized squid (cleaned and membrane removed, you can ask your fishmonger to do this)

Coating
200g polenta flour
1 tsp dried chilli flakes
50g fennel leaf (chopped)
2 eggs (beaten with a splash of milk)
plain flour

Chilli Jam
½ onion (finely diced)
8 vine tomatoes
2 red chillies (finely sliced with the seeds)
200g caster sugar

To Serve
crème fraiche
lemon wedges

Method

For the Coating
In a large bowl mix together the polenta flour, chilli flakes and fennel leaf then prepare a tray with plain flour and another tray with 2 eggs beaten with a splash of milk. Clean the squid then dip into the flour, then the egg, then into the polenta mix. This is to protect it and give a nice crunchy coating when it's fried.

For the Chilli Jam
Place all the ingredients into a saucepan and bring to the boil, then turn down to a simmer. Cook out until a jam-like consistency is reached, approx. 20–30 minutes.

To Serve
Deep fry the squid at 180°C for 4–5 minutes or until golden brown, then serve with crème fraiche, the chilli jam and a wedge of lemon.

SMOKED HADDOCK PANCAKE WITH A MORNAY SAUCE, PARMENTIER POTATOES AND GREEN VEGETABLES

SERVES 4

Ingredients

600g of smoked haddock
small knob of butter
olive oil
mature Cheddar (grated)

Mornay Sauce
½ onion studded with 1 bay leaf and 4 cloves
300ml milk
25g butter
25g plain flour
1 tbsp Dijon mustard
100g mature Cheddar
salt and pepper

Pancakes
250ml milk
2 eggs
100g plain flour
50g dill (chopped)
salt and pepper

Parmentier Potatoes
3–4 medium-sized potatoes (peeled and squared off)
100ml olive oil
50g butter
sprigs of thyme

Method

For the Mornay Sauce

Add the studded onion to the milk in a saucepan, then scald the milk (bring it almost to the boil then allow to cool down) and leave to infuse for 15 minutes. Once the infusion is done, remove the onion. In another pan melt the butter then, stirring constantly, add in the flour to form a roux. Once the roux is formed add in the infused milk a bit at a time until the sauce is a nice smooth consistency, stirring constantly to make sure of no lumps. Once the sauce is cooked out add the Dijon mustard and the mature Cheddar to finish the sauce. Season to taste.

For the Pancakes

Put all the ingredients into a bowl and either use a hand whisk or a small stick blender to incorporate the ingredients into a batter. Leave to settle for 20 minutes, then cook the pancakes in a crêpe pan over a medium heat. This should make about 6 pancakes.

For the Parmentier Potatoes

Preheat oven to 180°C / gas 4
Dice the potatoes and boil in salted water until soft, but still with a bit of bite. Drain once ready. Preheat a tray with the olive oil, the butter and some sprigs of thyme. Place the potatoes on the tray and bake in the oven at 180°C for about 10–15 minutes, turning occasionally.

To Finish

Preheat oven to 180°C/gas 4
Fry off the smoked haddock in a small knob of butter and a splash of olive oil. Flake most of the haddock into the sauce but reserve some for the top of the pancakes.
Take your pancakes and, for each one, put some of the smoked haddock sauce mixture into one of the corners, then fold over and over again to form a triangle. Top with the rest of the flaked haddock and some grated Cheddar. Bake in the oven for 8–10 minutes.
Serve with some fresh green vegetables.

DARK CHOCOLATE MOUSSE WITH RASPBERRY JELLY TOPPING AND RASPBERRY SORBET

SERVES 4

Ingredients

Dark Chocolate Mousse
40g dark chocolate (70% cocoa solids)
75g butter
30g cocoa powder
2 eggs (whites and yolks separated)
50g caster sugar
60ml double cream

Sponge Base
2 eggs (whites and yolks separated)
60g caster sugar
20g cocoa powder

Raspberry Jelly Topping
150ml water
50g caster sugar
50g raspberries
1 sheet of leaf gelatine

Raspberry Sorbet
100ml water
50g liquid glucose
50g caster sugar
200g raspberries

To Serve
whipped cream
raspberry coulis
fresh raspberries
mint leaves

Method

For the Dark Chocolate Mousse
Melt the chocolate, butter and cocoa powder in a bowl on top of a pan of boiling water, making sure the water does not touch the bowl. Set aside to cool slightly.
Next whisk the egg whites in a bowl with 25g of the caster sugar until stiff peaks are formed.
In another bowl whisk the egg yolks with the remaining 25g of caster sugar until doubled in volume and pale (you might want to use an electric whisk if you have one). Once the egg mixtures are ready, fold the egg yolk mixture into the chocolate mixture, then fold in the egg whites a third at a time. The mixture should be light in appearance and not lumpy. Finally whip the double cream to stiff peaks and fold through the chocolate mousse. Put into a container and into the fridge to set.

For the Sponge Base
Preheat oven to 180°C / gas 4
Whisk the egg whites in a bowl with 40g of the caster sugar until stiff peaks are formed. In another bowl whisk the egg yolks and the remaining 20g of caster sugar until doubled in volume and pale in appearance. Next add the cocoa powder into the egg yolk mixture and fold through. After this, fold in the egg white mixture, a third at a time, until a light batter is formed with no lumps. Bake on a greaseproof covered tray at 180°C for 5–8 minutes. Leave to cool.

For the Raspberry Jelly Topping
Soak the sheet of leaf gelatine in cold water until soft, remove from the water and squeeze out excess water. Boil the water and sugar until dissolved then add the raspberries and blend. Strain out the seeds by pushing through a sieve. Stir in the soaked leaf of gelatine and leave to cool or refrigerate for 10 minutes.

For the Raspberry Sorbet
Boil the water, liquid glucose and sugar until a syrup is made. Add the raspberries to the syrup, then blend the

mixture and strain out the seeds. Allow to cool then churn using an ice cream machine for approx. 5 minutes.

To Build the Mousse Cakes
Using a metal ring mould cut out 8 rounds of the sponge, then place 4 of them back into the bottom of your moulds. Place your chocolate mousse in a piping bag then pipe it on top of the sponge until halfway up the ring mould. Put the other sponge on top and fill up with the mousse leaving a small space at the top for the jelly. Refrigerate for 10 minutes then top with the cooled jelly.

To Serve
Transfer the mousse cakes onto plates and garnish with whipped cream, raspberry coulis, a few fresh raspberries and mint leaves.

NIARBYL RESTAURANT

Dalby IM5 3BR
01624 843300
www.niarbylcafe.com

I was born in Newcastle-Upon-Tyne where my interest in cooking began from an early age with my mum teaching me to bake cakes and make family meals together at home. Our favourites in particular at that time were scones, braised beef and corned beef hash.

When I finally left school at the age of 16 I went straight into catering college for one day a week. My placement was with Gardner Merchant (a catering franchise). After completing my training I quickly moved through the ranks and had the great opportunity of working in a Michelin Star restaurant. From this I moved into working in hotels. This took me across the country from Dundee to Dartford, finally settling on the Isle of Man.

I was drawn to the Island as I have always had a love of the sea and fishing. Some of my fondest memories are from fishing the North-East coast with my dad.

I began my career on the Island as a sous chef in the Mount Murray Hotel and Country Club. I became head chef within the year and spent 10 years there. In 2012 my tender was accepted by Manx National Heritage and my dream of owning my own business, and working right on the sea front, became a reality. Coastline Catering was born.

I feel very lucky to be based at Niarbyl, a place steeped in history and so close to the sea. One of my oldest friends since moving to the Island, Alan Kermode, is a local fisherman based at Niarbyl Bay. He supplies the restaurant with fresh lobster and crab caught from within a stones throw away! I enjoy nothing more than a day's fishing with Alan.

On a quiet day, my children and I take our kayaks out onto the bay to fish for pollock and mackerel for the restaurant. This is popular on our menu and has been served to celebrities such as Hugh Fearnley-Whittingstall.

The Isle of Man has a wealth of natural and farmed produce that is world renowned, from its queenies to its cheese. This is incorporated into our menus. I have come to consider a lot of the local suppliers as good friends and use their produce on our menu.

Looking to the future: we hope to grow the business. My son works full-time in the kitchen and my daughter helps out over holidays and weekends. We are a close family and I hope to inspire them to share the same passion for food and to work hard.

SEAFOOD CHOWDER

SERVES 4

Ingredients

2 sticks of celery
2 carrots
2 potatoes
1 onion
225g cod cod
225g salmon
1 tbsp olive oil
2 garlic cloves (crushed)
1 heaped tbsp plain flour
500ml milk
250ml double cream
250ml fish stock
113g prawns
225g queenies

To Serve
crusty bread
butter

Method
Dice the vegetables, cod and salmon, setting the vegetables and fish aside in separate bowls.

Next heat the oil in a saucepan, add the diced vegetables and crushed garlic then fry gently until cooked. Sprinkle over the flour, mix thoroughly and slowly add the milk, cream and fish stock. Simmer until thickened.

Finally add the diced cod and salmon, prawns and queenies and simmer for 2 minutes.

Serve with crusty bread and butter.

The Island Kitchen : Niarbyl Restaurant

POLLOCK AND CHIPS

SERVES 4

Ingredients

Chips
6 large potatoes
oil for frying

Fish
4 large pollock fillets (skinned and pin-boned)
1 jar of horseradish sauce
500g plain flour
500ml lager
oil for frying
sea salt and cracked pepper

For the Peas
1 knob of butter
1 bag of peas
juice of 1 lemon
sea salt and cracked pepper

To Serve
1 bottle of vinegar
1 lemon (cut into wedges)

Method

For the Chips
Peel and cut the potatoes to the desired size then steam or boil until fully cooked.
Drain, dry and deep fry until golden brown.

For the Fish
Place the pollock fillets on a tray and rub both sides with horseradish sauce.
Mix some of the flour and the lager together in a large bowl until a light batter is achieved.
Next dust the pollock fillets with the remaining flour and seasoning.
Coat the fish in the batter and deep fry until golden brown.

For the Peas
Heat the butter, then add the peas, lemon juice and salt and pepper to taste.
Simmer until the peas soften and crush with a masher.

To Serve
Serve all together with vinegar and fresh lemon wedges.

The Island Kitchen: Niarbyl Restaurant

LEMON CHEESECAKE WITH A MIXED BERRY COMPOTE
SERVES 4

Ingredients
Base
1 pack ginger nut biscuits
125g butter (softened)

Filling
200g Philadelphia cheese
150ml double cream
75g caster sugar
2 lemon juice

Berry Compote
½ punnet of raspberries
½ punnet of blueberries
½ punnet of strawberries
½ punnet of blackberries
75g caster sugar
1 shot (25ml) Cointreau

Method
For the Base
Tip the biscuits into a food processor and mix until they resemble a fine crumb.
Add the softened butter and mix again, then place into a greased cake tin, patting down to create a firm base, and set aside in the refrigerator to chill.

For the Filling
Mix the cheese and cream until it forms soft peaks. Add the sugar and lemon juice, and beat until smooth before placing on top of the biscuit mix. Leave to chill overnight.

For the Berry Compote
Place the berries, sugar and Cointreau in a saucepan and simmer until the fruit breaks down.
Chill overnight.

To Serve
Slice the cheesecake and serve with a dollop of the mixed berry compote.

THE ABBEY RESTAURANT

Rushen Abbey, Ballasalla, Isle of Man, IM9 3DB
01624 822 393
www.theabbeyrestaurant.co.im/

Situated next to the ruins of an ancient monastery, The Abbey restaurant is steeped in history. Originally built with stones reclaimed from Rushen Abbey in the C18th, this fine country house has evolved over the years into the beautiful restaurant it is today. At the heart of The Abbey's menu is the desire to showcase the very best of the Island's surroundings. The main focus each season is to bring together local artisans, farmers and foragers with our ever increasing home-grown offerings to invite the diner to savour a true taste of the Manx ground and air.

The Abbey Restaurant is a stylish, hidden gem set amid luscious green surroundings. Our large 140 cover dining room has a menu that changes daily, and which makes the best of the Island's seasonal produce, in the tradition of modern European cooking, with an accessible showcasing some of the world's finest wines and liqueurs. The Abbey is made up of four spaces which work together in perfect harmony: there are the two main restaurant areas, the garden room and the private dining room. Join us for a meal and discover relaxed fine dining at its best.

WILD RABBIT, LOCAL BLACK PIG AND FORAGED MUSHROOM TERRINE WITH MEDLAR JELLY

SERVES 4

Ingredients

Terrine
2 wild rabbits (prepared)
4 sage leaves
1 tbsp white truffle oil
2 ham hocks
350g wild mushrooms
1 tbsp butter
1 tbsp chervil (chopped)
1 tbsp parsley (chopped)
sea salt and black pepper

Medlar Jelly
1 kg medlars (or substitute with crab apples)
500g granulated sugar
peel of ½ lemon

To Serve
white truffle oil

Method
Prepare a terrine mould by lining it with cling film.

For the Terrine
Place all the parts of the rabbit, along with salt, pepper, sage leaves and the truffle oil, into a vacuum pack bag and seal well (your butcher will vac pac for you if you ask). Cook sous vide for 8 hours at 67⁰C. As an alternative you can confit the rabbit instead.
Using a large saucepan, boil the ham hocks in clean water, keeping well-covered, for 2 hours or until tender and falling away from the bone.
Wash the wild mushrooms well and pat dry with a towel, then fry in a little butter until golden and allow to cool.
Next, remove the ham hocks from the stock they have created and pick all of the meat from the bones – take care to remove all fat and sinew. Reserve the stock for later.
Remove the rabbit from sous vide, or confit oil, and pick all the meat from the bones.
Take 500ml of the stock from the ham and mix in the chopped herbs, then check for seasoning.
Taking the prepared terrine mould, layer the ingredients until they fill the terrine.
Pour over the herb stock until the meat and mushrooms are covered, then chill in the refrigerator for 3 hours.

For the Medlar Jelly
In a heavy-bottomed pan, cook the fruits gently until they form a soft pulp.
Place in a jelly bag overnight, over a clean pan in which to collect the dripping liquid.
Using 450g of sugar per 600ml of liquid collected, boil the mixture up with the lemon peel, skimming off impurities with a ladle as you go.
Pour the liquid into moulds, or a jar, and allow to cool.

To Serve
Slice the terrine onto a serving plate and spoon on some of the fresh medlar jelly. Drizzle with a little extra truffle oil and enjoy!

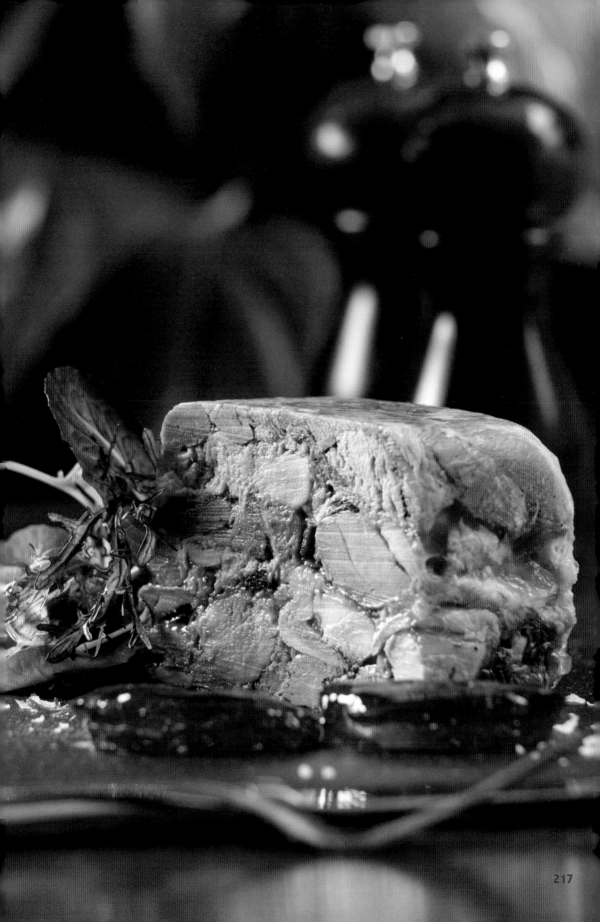

ROAST MALLARD BREAST, CONFIT LEG, CHESTNUT PURÉE, BLACKENED KOHLRABI, SQUASH SOUP

SERVES 4

Ingredients

Confit Legs
1 mallard
10g rock salt
3 cloves garlic
5 star anise
500g goose fat
salt and black pepper

Blackened Kohlrabi
6 various coloured kohlrabi (peeled and cubed)
100g Manx butter
300ml chicken stock
salt and black pepper

Squash Soup
500g local squash of any kind (cut into large chunks)
1 bunch of thyme
75g unsalted butter (diced)
1 large onion (finely chopped)
1 tbsp olive oil
500ml chicken stock
50ml Manx double cream

Chestnut Purée
1 orange (segmented and juice reserved)
10g unsalted butter
5g brown sugar
200g chestnuts
100ml chicken stock
50ml double cream
salt and black pepper

Mallard Breast
reserved crown of Mallard
1 tbsp olive oil

To Serve
First:
100g plain flour
1 egg (beaten)
⅔ handfuls of Panko breadcrumbs
80ml olive oil

Second:
100g cornflour
150g plain flour
10g baking powder
ice-cold water
2 tbsp sage leaves
vegetable oil for frying
1 tbsp pumpkin seeds (toasted)

Method

For the Confit Legs
Remove the legs from the mallard. Put in a dish, sprinkle with the rock salt, cover and chill for 12 hours.
Clean the rest of the bird, carefully removing the wishbone, and leave chilled for later.
Preheat oven to 140°C/gas 1
Rinse and dry the legs and put in an oven dish, into which they fit snugly, with the garlic and star anise. Melt the goose fat in a pan and then pour it over the legs. Cook in a covered pan for 2 ½ hours or until the meat is falling off the bone. Discard the skin, garlic and star anise and remove all the meat from the confit legs. Shred the meat and season lightly.
Layer the meat into a small tray to about 1cm thick, then chill until firm.

For the Blackened Kohlrabi
Place the cubed kohlrabi, butter and stock in a large heavy-bottomed saucepan, evenly spread

out. Season and cover with a lid.
Cook over a low heat for 20 minutes, turn over the kohlrabi and cook without a lid until the stock reduces. Allow the kohlrabi to crisp up in the pan. Reserve for plating.

For the Squash Soup
Preheat oven to 190°C/gas 5. Place the chopped squash, thyme and butter in a foil parcel. Bake for about 30 minutes or until soft. In a saucepan sweat the onion in a little oil until soft, then add the roasted squash flesh and stock. Bring to the boil, add the cream, then blend until completely smooth (thermomix is best). Pass through a fine sieve and adjust the seasoning.

For the Chestnut Purée
Caramelise the orange segments with the butter and sugar in a pan, being careful not to burn the sugar. Add the orange juice, peeled chestnuts and stock, bring to the boil and then blend until smooth. Slowly add the cream.
Pass through a fine sieve and adjust the seasoning.

For the Mallard Breast
Preheat oven to 200°C / gas 6
Season the mallard crown and then seal in a hot pan in 1 tablespoon of oil.

Roast for 10–15 minutes depending on the size of the bird and how well you like it cooked.
Allow to rest.
Carve off the mallard breasts once roasted, slicing each breast evenly.

To Serve
First:
Cut the confit leg meat into 1cm cubes and then dust with the flour, dip in the egg and coat with the breadcrumbs.
Shallow-fry the leg meat cubes until golden all over.

Second:
Mix the cornflour, plain flour and baking powder together in a bowl.
Gently add the ice-cold water, stirring gently until it forms a tempura batter.
Heat the oil in a deep-fat fryer.
Dip the sage leaves in the tempura batter and fry until the batter sets on the leaves.
Drain on kitchen paper.
Spoon a little chestnut purée onto each plate, add some mallard cubes, kohlrabi, and the mallard breast, top with pumpkin seeds and deep-fried sage leaves.
Pour the squash soup around the meat to serve.

POACHED PEAR, VANILLA CUSTARD, HONEY CREAM, GINGER CRUMB, PEAR SORBET, CANDIED WALNUT

SERVES 4

Ingredients

Poached Pear
2 ripe pears (peeled, halved)
1 vanilla pod
2 tbsp dark brown sugar
1 tbsp unsalted butter
pinch flaky sea salt

Vanilla Custard
325ml Manx double cream
100ml full-fat milk
1 vanilla pod (split in half)
50g golden caster sugar
6 free-range egg yolks

Honey Cream
2 tbsp Manx honey
300ml Manx double cream

Ginger Crumb
5 tbsp butter
½ tsp ground mace
½ tsp kosher salt
¼ tsp freshly grated nutmeg
1 inch piece ginger (peeled and grated)
140g plain flour

Pear Sorbet
4 ripe pears (peeled and quartered)
300g caster sugar
100ml water
1 star anise
1 stick cinnamon
½ lemon (sliced)

Candied Walnuts
60g icing sugar
¼ tsp cayenne pepper
200g walnut halves
pinch of salt

To Serve
Edible flowers

Method

For the Poached Pear
Set the souse vide to 79°C
Slice the pears in half lengthwise and scoop out the core.
Divide the pear halves between two zipper-lock or vacuum-seal bags.
Slice the vanilla pod in half lengthwise and use the back of a paring knife to scrape all of the seeds out into a small bowl. Add the brown sugar and salt.
Using your fingers, rub the vanilla seeds into the sugar until well combined.
Divide the sugar mixture between the two bags. Add ½ tablespoon of butter and one half of the vanilla pod to each bag.
Seal the bags using the water immersion technique or a vacuum sealer.
Transfer the bags to the water bath and set the timer for 30 minutes. As an alternative poach the pear halves in a little stock syrup until tender.

For the Vanilla Custard
Preheat oven to 110°C / gas ¼. Heat all the ingredients, except the egg yolks, in a heavy-bottomed pan until the sugar dissolves, taking care not to let the mixture boil. Mix the yolks well in a large bowl. Slowly add the hot mixture to the yolks, mixing all the time, then pass through a fine sieve. Pour into an ovenproof dish. Cook the custard by placing the dish in a tray of hot water in the oven for 30 minutes until almost set

(slightly wobbly). Remove from the tray and chill ready to use later.

For the Honey Cream
Whisk together the honey and double cream until almost reaching stiff peaks.

For the Ginger Crumb
Preheat oven to 180°C/gas 4
Blend the butter, mace, salt, nutmeg, and ginger in an electric mixer, then mix in the flour until small crumbles form. Place the crumb on a baking tray and bake in the oven for around 25 minutes until golden brown. Allow to cool.

For the Pear Sorbet
Place the pears in a freezer-safe container.
In a saucepan boil all the other ingredients together until a syrup is formed.
Pour the syrup over the pears, discarding all the other ingredients. Freeze until solid.
Break or cut into smaller pieces then blend well in a mixer until smooth. Keep in the freezer until plating.

For the Candied Walnuts
Preheat oven to 175°C / gas 4
Mix together all the ingredients in a bowl except the walnuts. Boil the walnuts in a pan for 3 minutes and drain well, then immediately roll in the sugar mixture. Bake in the oven until golden brown, stirring occasionally, taking care not to burn them. Cool completely before using.

To Serve
Smear a spoonful of honey cream across a chilled, presentable plate. Create two lines of ginger crumb in the opposite direction. Place two quenelles of custard onto the cream. Cut a pear half into four and place leaning on the custard quenelles. Place small quenelles of sorbet around the dish. Place dots of honey cream around using a piping bag. Finish with extra ginger crumb and edible flowers.

THE FORGE

Santon, Isle of Man, IM4 1JE
01624 610031
www.theforge.im

The Forge was born early in the spring of 2013, the spring of the snow! Just a few days after acquiring the keys in March, a hefty amount of snow hit the Isle of Man and for a few weeks the only way new owners Artan and Sarah Xhumrri, and their children, could visit the site was to park some way off and slip-slide down to the dilapidated gateway at the front of the building. This enforced closure allowed us time to really look at what we had invested in, seeing for the first time the potential of the beautiful grounds and surroundings.

We knew this site deserved to become something special, something true to its roots as an old Manx farm, something authentic.

We stripped the building back to the bones, and left it there; the interior has been restored using old fittings and fixtures from around the site. We were lucky to uncover some gems such as our slate mantles for above the fire places (discovered buried under the old front porch), old tools hidden in sheds, reclaimed timbers and wiring from the original site. Always respecting the environment and local ecosystem.

The Forge smokehouse and grill, with its crackling fires and large open-plan dining rooms, allows for leisurely family-style feasting in a totally unique and independent environment where quality and authenticity is at the heart of everything we do.

The offering at the Forge is simple. Grown from our Albanian and British market town roots, we make every dish fresh, local and from scratch on-site. Our menu has a spine of freshly prepared, classic grill dishes, complemented by Mediterranean influences: in other words, modern British cookery.

The food offering is based on marinating, slow cooking, grilling and smoking the best meat, fish and vegetables we can get our hands on. Very little is done after that, we dress it with our secret seasoning, extra virgin olive oil and freshly chopped flat-leaf parsley – home-grown whenever possible! You taste the quality of our local meat and seafood as nature intended. We have a passion to support our fellow local farmers and producers, and work closely with several expert farmers to maintain a quality supply in our restaurant.

When it comes to drinking, we hope to allow our guests to explore. Our botanical, crafted cocktails and infusions are the perfect way to soak up the flavoursome food offering. We have an eclectic wine boutique showcasing some of the world's best known types and producers, and we also source our Own Label house wines to be perfectly balanced with the food we create – and as always, our skilled and passionate team strive to uphold our authentic soul by working closely with the seasons, and each other, to deliver an utterly unique experience.

Wherever possible we grow our own, with budding gardens of herbs, flowers, fruit and vegetables. Our ketchup, butter and condiments are also homemade and our shop, both in-house and online, allows our guests to take a little of the Forge home to enjoy.

The root of the Forge hospitality is simply getting around the table together for the best of all things – eating, drinking and making merry!

SPINACH, MUSHROOM & GOAT'S CHEESE STRUDEL

SERVES 4

Ingredients

A knob of fresh butter or a couple of spoonfuls of good olive oil

1 banana shallot (peeled and diced)

2 cloves garlic (finely chopped)

400g Greeba Farm chestnut mushrooms (rinsed and sliced)

500g goats cheese

400g local or home-grown spinach (washed well) (this can easily be substituted for other seasonal leaves, such as Sheila Gawne rainbow chard or Staarvey Farm kale)

200g fresh breadcrumbs

a handful of fresh garden herbs (we love our home-grown parsley, thyme and rosemary)

sea salt and pepper

Pastry

225g plain flour

28g lard

100ml iced water

175g butter

pinch of salt

(or substitute for good quality shop-bought puff pastry)

1 egg (beaten)

Method

Heat the butter or oil in a pan and soften the shallot, garlic and mushrooms together, allowing a little colour to develop.

Toss in the washed spinach and wilt until completely soft. Next tip in the breadcrumbs and herbs, and mix well, taking care not to mash up the wilted spinach.

Set the mixture aside and allow to cool, during this time the breadcrumbs will soak up the delicious liquid from the mushrooms.

For the Pastry

Preheat oven to 200°C/gas 6

Blitz the flour, salt and lard in a food processor and spoon in water until a firm dough is formed. Of course old-school finger rubbing will get the job done... this is just a bit of a cheat that we think works just as well! Turn the dough out on to a floured surface and knead lightly until smooth. Chill in the fridge for 10 minutes.

Once chilled take the pastry out of the fridge and roll into a rectangle. Place the butter on the lower half of the rectangle and pat down to a similar size as the pastry using your rolling pin.

Fold over the pastry and roll out, then fold the pastry over at opposite ends (to meet in the middle) and roll out again. Chill in the fridge and repeat the process twice more.

To Finish

Roll out your puff pastry to around the size of an A4 sheet of paper and 6mm thick. Place on to a sheet of floured baking parchment in a landscape fashion (with the long end facing you).

Place the cooled spinach mix along the bottom of the pastry, place the goats cheese in the centre and then roll up the pastry like a sausage roll, using the baking parchment to help the process along. Pinch the 2 ends together to close the mixture inside.

Place the paper and strudel on to a baking sheet and glaze with a well-beaten egg or milk.

Bake in the oven for around 35 minutes or until golden brown all over.

To Serve

Serve slices straight from the oven or keep in the fridge for up to a week.

Try serving this with cheese or fresh pesto and salad as a delicious lunch dish.

SLOW ROAST MANX BRISKET

SERVES 4

Ingredients

907g joint of local brisket
1 large white onion (peeled and diced)
4 carrots (peeled and roughly chopped)
3 sticks of celery (sliced)
2 sprigs of rosemary
2 sprigs of thyme
6 bay leaf
6 cloves of garlic
pinch of cinnamon
400ml red wine
600g chopped tinned tomatoes
oil for frying
salt and pepper

To Serve
Your favourite rice, fries or creamy mash

Method

Preheat oven to 150°C/gas 2
In a heavy-bottomed pan, sear the well-seasoned beef
joint until brown on all sides.
Set the beef aside and brown all the vegetables, herbs
and the cinnamon in the remaining juices. Pour in the red
wine and reduce for 5 minutes, then add the chopped
tinned tomatoes and taste to check the seasoning.
Place the beef in a casserole dish or roasting tray and
pour over the mixture to cover. Cover with a lid and place
into a medium oven (around 150°C) for 6 hours.

To Serve
When the meat is soft it is ready to serve and is great
served with rice, fries or creamy mash – enjoy!

BOOZY PECAN PIE

SERVES 4

Ingredients

450g sweet shortcrust pastry
110g butter
1 vanilla pod (seeds only)
225g muscovado sugar
110g golden syrup
4 eggs
20ml Celtic Mist (or bourbon)
285g pecans

To Serve
cream or ice cream of your choice

Method
Preheat oven to 180°C/gas 4
Line an 8 inch cake tin or flan ring with the shortcrust pastry and bake blind for 15 minutes.
Cook the butter, vanilla, sugar and syrup in a large saucepan until the sugar is dissolved and the mixture begins to boil, then remove from the heat and allow to cool a little (roughly 15 minutes).
Turn down the oven slightly to 175°C
Once the sugar and butter mixture is cooled pour in the eggs, alcohol and pecans and stir well.
Pour the mixture into the pastry case and bake in the oven at 175°C for 35–40 minutes.

To Serve
Serve the warm pecan pie with cream or ice cream.

CASTLETOWN AND THE SOUTH

LEONARDO'S

Stanley House, Castletown.
01624 827635
www.facebook.com/Leonardosrestaurantiom

If you are visiting Castletown, the ancient capital of the Island, you may notice an Italian restaurant opposite Castle Rushen. In the shadow of the castle you can get the best Italian food presided over by Head Chef, Angiolino. The other chefs that work in Leonardo's come from all over the Mediterranean including Italy, Morocco, Spain, Cyprus and Portugal – all giving their unique and special twist to their food. Nowhere else in the world would you find so much of the Mediterranean in the shadow of a medieval castle.

Ben Batoul, the proprietor of Leonardo's, has worked in the catering industry for a number of years. Born in Morocco to a Spanish mother and a Moroccan father, he was brought up in Brussels and trained there to be a chef. He has worked in various prestigious establishments all over the world including working in Paris, Bermuda, Brussels and working aboard Cunard's *Queen Elizabeth 2*.

During the construction of this fabulous new restaurant builders uncovered an old Renaissance period water well, which can be viewed when trying the Mediterranean inspired cuisine. While you are there you may notice that the staff are all dressed to impress, and their service reflects that!

Appetising recipes from the Isle of Man's finest chefs and restaurants

FIGS AND HALLOUMI IN CINNAMON AND HONEY

SERVES 4

This recipe can be served either as a starter or a dessert; simply leave out the halloumi and replace the rocket and prosciutto with yogurt if serving as a dessert.

Ingredients

12 figs (not too ripe)
4 tsp brown sugar
4 tbsp cinnamon
4 tbsp Parmesan cheese (grated)
4 tbsp butter
16 pieces of halloumi
2 tbsp white wine
12 tbsp honey
12 slices of prosciutto
olive oil

To Serve

50g rocket leaves

Method

Preheat oven to 200°C/gas 6
First clean your figs with a little of olive oil, then halve lengthwise.
Place a few drops of oil into a baking dish and place the figs inside. Sprinkle the fig halves with brown sugar and cinnamon then a little Parmesan and finally dot each fig with the butter.
Place the halloumi slices around the figs, and glaze the dish with the white wine.
Bake in the oven at 200°C for around 10 minutes.

To Serve

Drizzle the honey on top of the baked figs, halve the prosciutto slices and arrange on top of each fig in the shape of a flower.
Serve on a bed of rocket leaves.

SUPREME OF CHICKEN IN A COFFEE SAUCE
SERVES 4

Ingredients

4 chicken breasts
4 tsp butter
4 tsp dark brown sugar
8 tsp Tia Maria
salt and pepper to taste

Marinade
4 espresso shots (120ml)
4 tbsp balsamic vinegar
4 tbsp dark brown sugar
4 tbsp extra virgin olive oil
8 cloves of garlic (minced)
8 tsp crushed black pepper
pinch of salt

For the Sauce
4 espresso shots
double cream

To Serve
rosemary mashed potato

Method

For the Marinade
Stir together the espresso, balsamic vinegar, brown sugar, olive oil, garlic, black pepper and a little salt. Butterfly the chicken breast and marinate the chicken for at least ½ hour.

For the Chicken
Once marinated, season the chicken with salt and pepper and roast on both sides in a frying pan with the butter, over a medium heat, until cooked through. Sprinkle the chicken with the dark brown sugar and allow briefly to caramelise, then flambé with the Tia Maria.

For the Sauce
Reduce 4 espresso shots with double cream until the sauce reaches the consistency, and potency, you prefer.

To Serve
Plate the chicken with the sauce and serve on a bed of rosemary mashed potato.

As an Alternative
If you are short of time and would prefer not to marinate your chicken:
Gently sauté the minced garlic with the olive oil. Add the brown sugar, then add the espresso shots, the balsamic vinegar and butter. Roast the chicken in the sauce in a frying pan, over a medium heat, until cooked through. Finally flambé with the Tia Maria.
Serve on a bed of rosemary mashed potato, pouring the cooking sauce over the chicken.

MANDARIN CHEESECAKE (NON-COOK)

SERVES 4

Ingredients

24 digestive biscuits (crushed, for crumb base)
450g butter (melted)
900g white sugar
1.8kg cream cheese
4 tsp vanilla flavouring
zest of one orange
4 tbsp Cointreau
4 fresh mandarins (peeled and pitted, cut into segments)
480ml fresh orange juice

Loose-bottomed or spring-clipped tin, greased

Method

In a large bowl, crush the biscuits with the melted butter and a teaspoon of the sugar. Mix well then place into the base of your tin, patting down firmly. Refrigerate while you make the filling.

Combine the remaining sugar, cream cheese, vanilla flavouring, orange zest and the Cointreau until a creamy consistency is achieved and the sugar has dissolved into the mix. Take the tin out of the fridge and spoon the mixture over the biscuit base. Return to the fridge to set for 20 minutes.

Finally, take the fresh mandarin and place in a saucepan with the orange juice, gently bring to a simmer and reduce until the liquid forms a sticky glaze. Once the cheesecake is set, place the mandarin segments on top and spoon over the glaze.

Return to the fridge and allow to set for 3 hours before removing from the tin and serving.

The Island Kitchen : Leonardo's

PATCHWORK IS PASSIONATE
IN SUPPORTING LOCAL
SUPPLIERS...
WE ♥ QUALITY MANX
PRODUCE...
WE DON'T USE PROCESSED
FOODS...
OUR LOCAL
SUPPLIERS ARE :-
√ COOIL BROTHERS
√ THE EGG MAN
√ RADCLIFFE'S
√ KALLOW POINT SEAFOODS
√ LAXEY GLEN MILLS
√ RAMSEY BAKERY
√ HARRISON & GARRETT
√ PADDY'S √COCOA RED
√ CARRICK BAY SEAFOODS
√ APPLE ORPHANAGE
√ ISLE OF MAN CREAMERIES
√ RHUBARB MAN
√ GREEN MANN SPRINGS
√ ELLERSIE FARM
√ STAARVEY FARM
√ ROBINSONS
√ SHOPRITE
√ LOCAL ALLOTMENT
   HOLDERS- YOU KNOW WHO
   YOU ARE!

Patchwork Homemade
Chutneys & Jams.
Freshly made for you to
take away.

Water
spray

CHAPTER 4

QUIRKY AND SMALLER ESTABLISHMENTS ON THE ISLAND

There are many smaller establishments scattered around the Island but what they lack in size they make up for with their unique qualities. Cafés, guesthouses and tea rooms, all producing excellent food and drink, can often be overlooked in favour of the larger restaurants, but do so and you're missing out.

Lovingly crafted meals are delivered with the same quality and attention to detail as the larger establishments, often within quirky, cosy, beautiful or out-of-the-way places. Boutique bars, cute cafés, artisan bakers and historic buildings add a personal touch to the dining experience. Using the highest-quality, locally-sourced ingredients these establishments should definitely be on your go-to list when something less formal is required.

PORT ST MARY

THE LITTLE BIRD CAFE *

Port St Mary, Isle of Man IM95AE
Facebook: https://www.facebook.com/LittleBirdYpsi/

We stumbled across a little cafe in beautiful Port St Mary, right down in the sunny south of the Isle of Man, in April 2011 and straight away knew it was the perfect spot to begin our foodie quest. Having dreamt about our own cafe for years, we pulled together all our favourite things from our round-the-world travels and mixed them up with the British seaside cafe. We wanted to keep stalwart classics such as the full breakfast and cheese on toast, but revamp them using Manx produce on offer from local farmers, allotment holders, fisherman, roadside honesty boxes, and basically anywhere we could find the good stuff!

So we insisted on local pork butcher's sausages, free-range farm eggs (thanks Eggman!), homemade soda bread and Greeba mushrooms for the Full Manx breakfasts with Manx Cheddar, homemade chutneys and home-cooked ham for our rarebits.

However simple the menu item, we loved to spin things around and give it a bit of 'special lovin'!

Thankfully friends, local families and visitors from across liked what we were doing and word spread of our motto 'Always Homemade' and quickly we became packed with guests ordering up Loaghtan burgers, vintage picnics to take away and our famous homemade chips.

The year we opened our two daughters Alannah and Ciara were still in high school, so we would juggle our commitments in the kitchen with homework, lifts to friends' houses and sleepovers, which usually concluded with a stream of sleepy teenagers having breakfast in the cafe the morning after. Looking back I guess it was inevitable that we would become a real family orientated, community cafe.

By 2014 our tiny kitchen was bursting at the seams and we needed somewhere bigger to make all our cakes. That's when we converted the old bakery in the back of Patchwork into a full-size professional kitchen; that's when things really started to take off.

Looking back on our humble beginnings, we reflect that we really could not have done it without our loyal customers, our amazing staff, friends and family, who are often always keen helpers, especially when it comes to tasting the latest cakes!

* Due to open early 2017

BAY NY CARRICKEY CHOWDER

SERVES 4

Ingredients

1 small white onion
3 sticks celery (well diced)
70g salted butter
70g plain Laxey flour
300ml dry Martini/vermouth
650ml full-fat milk
300g brown crab meat
100g white crab meat
750g cold smoked Callig (2cm diced)
250g Manx queenies
350g sweetcorn (frozen)

To Serve

parsley (finely chopped)
lemon juice
Tabasco sauce (optional)

Method

Sweat off the onion and celery in the butter over a low heat until soft and translucent.

With a wooden spoon or spatula, continuously stir in 70g of plain Laxey flour to begin making a roux.

Still over a low heat, stir in the Martini and allow to thicken to a sauce before slowly pouring in the full-fat Manx milk. Bring back to the simmer.

Add all the crab meat, breaking up with the spatula so as to avoid lumps, followed by the diced smoked Callig (2cm dice is fine).

Manx queenies go in next and finally the frozen sweetcorn.

Bring the whole pot back to a gentle 10 minute simmer, taking care to lift the sweetcorn off the bottom of the pan where it is inclined to settle and burn if unattended.

Finally add milk or water to loosen and achieve a light chowder-type consistency.

(If your chowder is too thin you can add mashed potatoes to thicken).

To Finish

Add a handful of finely chopped parsley and a generous squeeze of lemon juice and serve immediately.

Optional Extras

A glug of Tabasco works very well if you like piquancy. We like to serve with our homemade soda or sourdough bread or you can hollow out any rustic loaf and serve the chowder using the bread as a serving vessel.

LAXEY

THE CRAFTEA WEAVER TEAROOM

Laxey Woollen Mills, Glen Road, Laxey IM4 7AR
01624 863373/860330
www.presenceofmann.com/tearoom

The historic Woollen Mills in Laxey, home to the two Manx tartans, was originally Moughtin's Corn Mill. It became a weaving mill in 1879 when it was converted with the help of investment by The Guild of St George, whose founder, John Ruskin, was to make a friend of Egbert Rydings, the new owner of the mill. To honour the Guild's faith in him, Egbert abided by four rules set down by Ruskin: all materials used should be of the best and purest quality; that finished goods must be 'as perfect as fingers can make them'; that anyone should be able to buy pure wool products direct from the mill, and finally 'no credit – it will save sleepless nights'.

The mill has been in the present family since 1949 and supports two full-time weavers using both a traditional loom built in 1926 and a modern pedal-loom. The large looms can still be seen up in the gallery and are still used. The mill has been exporting homemade cloth to Japan's high-end fashion industry over the last few years and is also home to The Hodgson Loom Art Gallery where exhibitions change monthly and the Presence of Mann gift shop, which sells quality Manx themed gifts that are shipped all over the world.

Opened in 2012, The CrafTea Weaver Tearoom is a tribute to John Wood the mill's Master Weaver.

The tearoom has locally-made quality crafts for sale, such as cushions and teddy bears, hence Craft in the name. Tea is served in proper china cups with teapots wearing hand-knitted tea cosies. Everything is for sale from the crockery to the tables and chairs.

Apart from possibly the largest selection of homemade cakes on the Island (up to 20 different cakes are usually available, including the famous Manx fruit bonnag), the tearoom has quickly gained a reputation for serving traditional, thick, Manx Broth with true plain bonnag. You can always tell a true Manxie – they don't have to ask what bonnag is. Also popular are the Weavers and Warpers salad platters.

MANX BROTH SERVED WITH PLAIN BONNAG

SERVES 4

Ingredients

½ mug pearl barley
good quality meat stock
¼ mug brisket or shin beef (diced)
¼ mug knuckle of ham (diced)
¼ mug mutton (diced, Loaghtan will give the best flavour
and is less fatty)
½ mug cabbage (chopped)
½ mug turnip (diced)
½ mug carrots (diced)
½ mug leeks (sliced)
2 sticks celery (chopped)
parsley
pinch of thyme
salt and pepper

Method

Soak the barley overnight. Using a good quality meat
stock, cook together with the meat and vegetables on the
top of the cooker over a low heat for at least 3 hours.
Check frequently that it does not boil dry. Add the herbs
and check seasoning. Serve thick and hot with a good
chunky slice of plain bonnag.

BONNAG ACCOMPANIMENT

To make one loaf (one loaf is never enough)

Ingredients

225g Manx flour
25g lard or vegetable fat
½ tsp carbonate of soda
½ tsp salt
¼ tsp cream of tartar
150ml buttermilk or sour milk

Method

Preheat oven to 180⁰C/gas 4

Mix well all the dry ingredients and the vegetable fat or
lard. Make into a dough with the milk, form into shape
(traditionally a flattish round but a loaf tin will be fine)
and bake either directly on the shelf, or in a loaf tin, in a
moderate oven for approx. ¾ hour or until cooked.

DOUGLAS

THE TICKETHALL

Douglas Railway Station, Bank Hill, Douglas IM1 4LL
01624 627888
www.ticket-hall.com

Down at Douglas Steam Railway Station on the North Quay, the tradition of cooking food on the footplate of a steam train has been kept alive by Steve Quirke and the team, in the Tickethall restaurant.

The fine art of cooking bacon, sausage and everything else for a full English breakfast that is served upon a fireman's shovel is still a common practice. Back in the day the cooking and serving of a breakfast with nothing more than a shovel to cook with was one of the fireman's jobs;

his day would start with arriving early, at the crack of dawn, to prepare the locomotive for its day's work on the Isle of Man's Douglas to Port Erin line.

At the Tickethall we source ingredients from local farms in the belief that using local produce, where possible, is vitally important to the growth and longevity of local businesses. For example we use Greeba Farm for our mushrooms, Harrison & Garret from Ballahig Farm for our sausage and bacon and Juan Howland's free-range eggs.

THE TICKETHALL'S FIREMAN'S BREAKFAST

SERVES 1

Ingredients

2 Ballahig Farm finest pork sausages
1 ripe tomato
2 tbsp butter
2–3 rashers dry-cured bacon
2 hash browns
3–4 Greeba Farm button mushrooms
baked beans
2 Juan Howland's free-range eggs
2 slices of bread

To Serve

parsley (chopped)

Method

Preparation 5 minutes, cook 20 minutes, ready in 25 minutes.

Preheat oven to 220°C/gas 7

In a frying pan, brown the sausages on all sides over a medium heat and cook for 5 minutes. Transfer to a baking dish then bake the sausages in the oven for 10 minutes. Next score a cross into the bottom of the tomato and place, cross-side up, in the baking dish with the sausages. Bake both for 8 minutes. Turn off the oven, but do not remove the sausages and tomato.

Meanwhile, in the frying pan used to brown the sausages, melt a tablespoon of butter and fry the bacon, hash browns and the mushrooms over a high heat for 7 minutes until the mushrooms have softened, the bacon begins to crisp and the hash browns turn golden. Transfer to the oven to keep warm.

Heat the beans in a small saucepan over a medium heat, stirring frequently.

Finally, fry the eggs with the yolk unbroken to desired consistency and toast the bread. Use the remainder of the butter to spread over the toast.

On a warm serving plate, bring together the sausages, hash browns, bacon, beans, tomato, mushrooms, fried

eggs and toast. Season well, garnish with parsley and serve immediately.

Tip

Timing really is the biggest hurdle to get over for this dish. You want everything ready at the same time and hot, so use the oven as a place to keep things warm and remember to cook things like eggs and toast last.

DOUGLAS

THE ALPINE CAFE

5 Regent Street, Douglas, Isle of Man IM1 2EB
01624 619249
www.thealpinecafe.com

The Alpine is a super-cute café in Douglas. We specialise in healthy salads, nutritious soups, chunky sandwiches, big breakfasts and tasty cakes. Every weekend the café transforms into a pop-up restaurant with an ever-changing menu. We do everything from Soul Food to Caribbean, French to Turkish. Whatever's in season, whatever's tasty, whatever tickles our (and your) fancy.

The Alpine is run by husband and wife team Melanie and Simon, along with their lovely staff. Melanie spent her childhood summers in Portugal, riding on the back of mopeds, seeking out the best places to pick the juiciest peach or hunting for razor clams on remote beaches. That education in finding the tastiest ingredients has informed the philosophy of The Alpine. We make the food we love to eat ourselves. Everything is fresh, local wherever possible and designed to make you feel good.

Everyone loves our salads so we wanted to share one of our favourites with you here. We hope you enjoy it!

ROAST MANX CARROT, FENNEL AND FLAT-LEAF PARSLEY SALAD

SERVES 4

Ingredients

1kg Manx carrots
5 tbsp extra virgin olive oil
2 tsp Maldon salt
2 tbsp dried chilli flakes
2 tbsp cumin seeds
2 heads of fennel (finely sliced)
1 large red onion (finely sliced)
2 cloves of garlic (crushed)
2 tbsp red wine vinegar
1 large handful flat-leaf parsley (roughly chopped)

Method

Preheat oven to 190°C/gas 5
Get a baking tray ready.
Peel your carrots, wash well then slice into diagonals about 2cm thick and tip into your baking tray.
Add the olive oil, salt, chilli flakes, cumin seeds and mix.
Bake for one hour until tender and a little scorched in places.
Let your carrots cool for about 15 minutes and then tip everything into a bowl that is big enough to hold all your other ingredients.
Add the fennel, onion, garlic, red wine vinegar and parsley then turn together carefully and you are done!

PORT ST MARY

AARON HOUSE TEA ROOM

Aaron House, The Promenade, Port St Mary, Isle of Man, IM9 5DE
01624 835702
www.aaronhouse.co.uk

Aaron House is a 5* Guest House overlooking the beautiful chapel bay of Port St Mary. Apart from their beautifully decorated and truly authentic guest rooms, Aaron House is renowned for their indulgent afternoon teas. All of their afternoon teas reflect the very best of local, Manx produce and are prepared daily by a team who are passionately dedicated to their craft. The team at Aaron House have spent many years perfecting this quintessentially English tradition and have blended it with their head baker's outstanding knowledge of Swiss pastries and confectionery. These outstanding afternoon teas are all presented with a glamorous sense of tradition and occasion and are served in an atmospheric Victorian dining room. They feature a tantalising selection of finger sandwiches, tempting handcrafted savouries and an assortment of the finest patisseries, scones and fresh chocolates. They are also served with a delightful variety of premium teas and coffee. Enjoying an afternoon tea at Aaron House is a splendid way to pass an afternoon. Their tea room is also fully licensed.

To reserve a table please telephone 01624 835702. Please note that only advanced pre-bookings are accepted. No walk in service is provided.

MANX HOMITY PIE

SERVES 6

Ingredients

Homity Pie Filling
300g potatoes (peeled and diced)
110g Manx white onion (chopped)
170g Manx Vintage Cheddar
2 tbsp Manx cream
1 large Manx garlic clove or 1 tbsp wild garlic (chopped)
1 heaped tsp wholegrain mustard
1 Manx egg (lightly whisked)
butter for frying

Cheese Pastry
200g Manx plain flour
a pinch dry mustard
a pinch cayenne pepper
100–125g Manx butter (see Note)
100g Manx cheese (finely grated)
1 Manx egg yolk
1–2 tbsp cold water
flour for rolling out

Method

For the Homity Pie Filling
Boil the potatoes in salted water until just cooked. Drain well when ready.
Cook the onions slowly in a small amount of butter (do not brown) and add these to the potatoes.
Add all of the other ingredients to the potatoes and onions and lightly mix until all of the filling is combined.

For the Cheese Pastry
Preheat oven to 180°C/gas 4 to 200°C / gas 6 (depending on your oven)
Sift the flour and seasonings together into a bowl, then rub in the butter until the mixture resembles fine breadcrumbs. **Note** – use the smaller quantity of fat if the cheese is fatty and crumbly, the larger if it is fine and dry.
Add the cheese, egg yolk, and enough cold water to form a stiff dough.
Roll out on a lightly floured surface and use as required. Line 6 individual tartlet tins or 1 large tartlet tin with the cheese pastry and fill with the Homity Pie filling.
Bake for 30–40 minutes at 180°C–200°C (depending on the oven).

DOUGLAS

NOA BAKEHOUSE

Fort Street, Douglas, Isle of Man IM1 2LJ
01624 618063
www.facebook.com/Noa-Bakehouse

Noa is a sourdough bakehouse producing up to 250 loaves a day, as well as bagels, baguettes, pastries and cakes. Supplying to Island-based Shoprite Supermarket, and some of the best local restaurants, there is a bread revolution that is spreading!

Noa use the baking techniques of our ancestors, the purest most time-consuming methods, in order to produce a loaf free from commercial/processed yeast or any other nasty.

The bakehouse café offers a unique opportunity to try local, handcrafted produce in an industrial setting, with a view of the bakers, cooks and baristas.

NOA CHOCOLATE BROWNIE

SERVES 4

Ingredients

250g good quality chocolate (70% cocoa solids)
250g unsalted butter
300g golden caster sugar
3 large eggs, plus 1 extra egg yolk (lightly beaten)
60g plain flour (sifted)
½ tsp baking powder
pinch of salt
60g good quality cocoa powder

Method

Preheat oven to 180ºC/gas 4
Line a 23cm x 23cm baking tin with baking parchment.
Set a bowl over, but not touching, a pan of simmering water and add 200g of the chocolate. Allow to melt and then remove immediately.
Meanwhile, beat the butter and sugar together until light and fluffy. Break the rest of the chocolate into chips and set these aside.

With the mixer still running, gradually add the eggs to the butter and sugar mixture, beating well between each addition before pouring in any more. Mix on a high speed for 5 minutes until the batter has a silky sheen, and has increased in volume.

Remove the bowl from the mixer and gently fold in the melted chocolate and chocolate chips with a metal spoon, followed by the sifted flour, baking powder, salt, and cocoa powder.

Spoon the mixture into the tin, and bake for 30 minutes. Test with a skewer; it should come out sticky, but not coated with raw mixture. If it does, put it back into the oven for another 3 minutes, then test again. Prepare a roasting tin of iced water.

When the brownies are ready, remove the tin from the oven and place in the cold water bath, making sure that no water touches the cooked brownies.

Leave to cool for an hour before cutting into squares.
Store in an airtight container; they're even better next day.

CHAPTER 5
ENJOYING THE DRINKS OF THE ISLE OF MAN

Although the Island is renowned for its high quality cuisine, visitors and residents can also enjoy drinks that are unique to the Isle of Man. The long-standing tradition of brewing on the Island has a reputation for transparency due to the Pure Beer Act of 1874. You will always know what is in your pint if it is brewed on the Island, as the Act, which is still in force, requires by law that nothing other than water, malt, sugar and hops goes into a brew, unless it is approved by Tynwald. This allows Manx breweries to create new varieties of drink, but within strict guidelines. Your beer is as pure as beer can be.

Besides beers and ciders, which are showcased at the annual Isle of Man Beer and Cider Festival, the Island produces the finest pure spring water, fruit juices and pressés, vodka, and even tea and coffee blends. Whatever your preference there will be a drink for you.

DOUGLAS

BATH & BOTTLE

6 Victoria Street, Douglas, Isle of Man, IM1 2LH
01624 845400
www.bathandbottle.com

Bath & Bottle is an original and boutique cocktail bar where friends can meet and drink indulgent cocktails. The atmosphere at this glamorous throwback to Prohibition era drinking is pure nostalgia. Staff are immaculately attired, knowledgeable and passionate about their subject and a range of vintage and rare spirits indulges those with curiosity for new drinks.

We create expertly-built classic cocktails along with our very own house creations. We only use fresh ingredients in our drinks to ensure the highest quality.

One of our house creations is a twist on the classic Clover Club using ingredients from our fantastic local producers, Stephen and Jenny Devereau from Staarvey Farm.

STAARVEY CLUB

Ingredients

4 fresh raspberries (when in season or Staarvey Farm raspberry jam)
3 sprigs of Staarvey Farm thyme
40ml gin (we use Hendricks but feel free to use your favourite bottle)
20ml Dolin dry vermouth
egg white from 1 Staarvey Farm egg
20ml lemon juice
10ml sugar syrup
ice cubes

Method

Muddle 3 of the raspberries in your mixing glass and add thyme leaves from 2 of the sprigs before adding the remaining ingredients. Shake the mixture with 1 ice cube until the egg froths. Add more ice and shake vigorously until cold. Taste the drink to ensure it is balanced, adding more sugar syrup or lemon juice if needed. Double strain the drink into an elegant coupette and garnish with a raspberry that has been speared with the final sprig of thyme.

BUSHY'S BREWERY

Bushy's Brewery Ltd., Mount Murray, Braddan, Isle of Man IM4 1JE
01624 661244 (brewery)
01624 611101 (office)
www.bushys.com

Bushy's Brewery celebrated two milestones in 2015: it is 30 years since the first brews took place beneath the old Bushy's pub at the bottom of Victoria Street in Douglas in 1985 and it's the 25th anniversary of opening our full-blown brewery out at Mount Murray in 1990.

The original brewery was set up by former chef Martin Brunnschweiler with a lot of help from family friend and retired brewer the late Peter Cole (J.W.Lees, Thwaites, Yates & Jackson), who was developing a mini brewery with the students at Lancaster University. After an initial site visit to evaluate the feasibility of putting his equipment in the (tidal flooding!) cellars of Bushy's Bar and designing a suitable framework and platform to accommodate it (expertly built by builder Mick Holgate and joiner John 'Dog' Collister), Peter brought the plant over on the ferry and took Martin through some initial trial brews to find the ideal style of brew to appeal to the regulars in the pub – with the still popular Old Bushy Tail being born.

The first beer went on sale in January 1986 with one pump simply dispensing the single brew into the bar directly above the fermenters and with licensee, and sister, Nicky Brunnschweiler and experienced barmaid Mary Broderick given the task of introducing drinkers in the pub to the new ale on offer. It was thankfully well received and soon gained a loyal following, but being on the strong side (4.5% ABV) it didn't suit all tastes, so within six months Bushy's Bitter (3.8% ABV) was introduced and being more of a 'session' beer this widened the appeal to quaffers looking for a less intense product.

At the time that Bushy's fledgling brewery was starting up there were two established breweries on the Island – the older and more popular Castletown Brewery (35 pubs) and the larger Okell's with exactly double the estate at 70 pubs. To an outsider it seemed that Castletown were the more ambitious of the two, investing in new brewery equipment, revamping their pubs and having the far busier establishments in all towns, so it came as some surprise when Okell's made the move to take their rivals over. The result of the 'merger' was the closure of the historic Castletown Brewery and a (virtual) monopoly of pubs on the Island with the newly formed Isle of Man Breweries.

Bushy's involvement during this chapter was shaped when the newly merged company decided to put around 25 of their pubs up for sale – a move which persuaded Martin to expand the brewing operation to try and take advantage of these potential new customers.

Again with huge help from Peter Cole, a top-notch brewery plant was identified in Brighton (which had been owned by The Raven Brewery) and the snap decision was made to purchase the equipment before it was shipped off to the USA where a rival

purchaser lurked. The next problem was where to house the new brewery – the equipment sat in storage in England until the current site at Braddan was found and converted to its new use, and it was in September 1990 that world-renowned beer expert Michael 'Beerhunter' Jackson cut the ribbon as guest of honour at the official opening.

In the intervening years Bushy's has become the Island's most innovative brewery, under the watchful eye of Neil 'Curly' Convery who, along with his team, has passed milestones such as:

1) Becoming the IOM's first, and currently only, brewer of lager
2) Becoming the IOM's first brewer of wheat beer
3) Becoming the IOM's first brewer of fruit beer (Bramble)
4) Being 25 years since reviving the legendary Oyster Stout
5) Brewing by far the IOM's largest range of seasonal and commemorative brews
6) Bushy's championed the retaining of the IOM's historic Pure Beer Act in 1995, when the government and Okell's proposed its abolition.

Bushy's have a whole host of new ideas in the pipeline and are looking forward to the next 25 years – CHEERS!

THE SHORE HOTEL BREW PUB

Shore Hotel Brew Pub, Old Laxey Hill, Isle of Man IM4 7DA
01624 861509

The Shore Hotel is the only public house in Old Laxey; it adjoins the River Laxey, having a 150m beer garden with river frontage and is just two minutes from the harbour and beach. We opened for business in April 1990 after completely renovating the bar area and changing the old Stable Bar into the Chartroom Restaurant.

In 1996 a group of local residents formed the Old Laxey Brewing Company and the Chartroom Restaurant closed for good. We commissioned Non Ferrous Fabrications Ltd from Ringwood in Hampshire to design and install a 5 brl micro-brewing plant and production commenced in February 1997.

We are the smallest independent brewery on the Island and we only brew one cask conditioned beer, Bosun Bitter ABV 3.8%. The pub bar has a nautical theme and hence our beer was christened as 'Bosun Bitter'. The Old Laxey brewery is the only brewery on the Island with its own dedicated Tap Bar which has a full public licence. Brewery tours and private parties can be arranged by contacting Paul Phillips on 07624 336362 (mobile) or 01624 861509 (pub).

Home-cooked food is served in the bar and outside beer garden midday to 2.30 p.m., and 5 p.m. to 8 p.m. during summer months. The kitchen is generally closed during January and February but for the rest of the year, Tuesday evening (6 p.m. to 8 p.m.) is Curry Night where a choice of three curries is served with poppadum and pickles, naan bread, onion bhaji, vegetable samosa and boiled rice for £7.95. Thursday Night Steak has proved to be very popular and we are often fully booked. We serve a 10oz sirloin steak (trimmed), onion rings, mushrooms, tomatoes, chips and peas for £12.95. We also provide a blue cheese or pepper sauce; the latter has proved very popular. A new advent, on a Saturday afternoon/evening, is our 8oz steak burger meal, served on a 5in floured bap with a salad garnish and chips.

This summer we have created two en-suite bedrooms for B&B, both have double beds with a small lounge area to one end, tea and coffee making facilities and a mini bar. The rooms have windows on three sides and are on the top floor, so have a lovely view overlooking the harbour or a mountain view to the rear. Breakfast is served in the room at a small table and chairs.

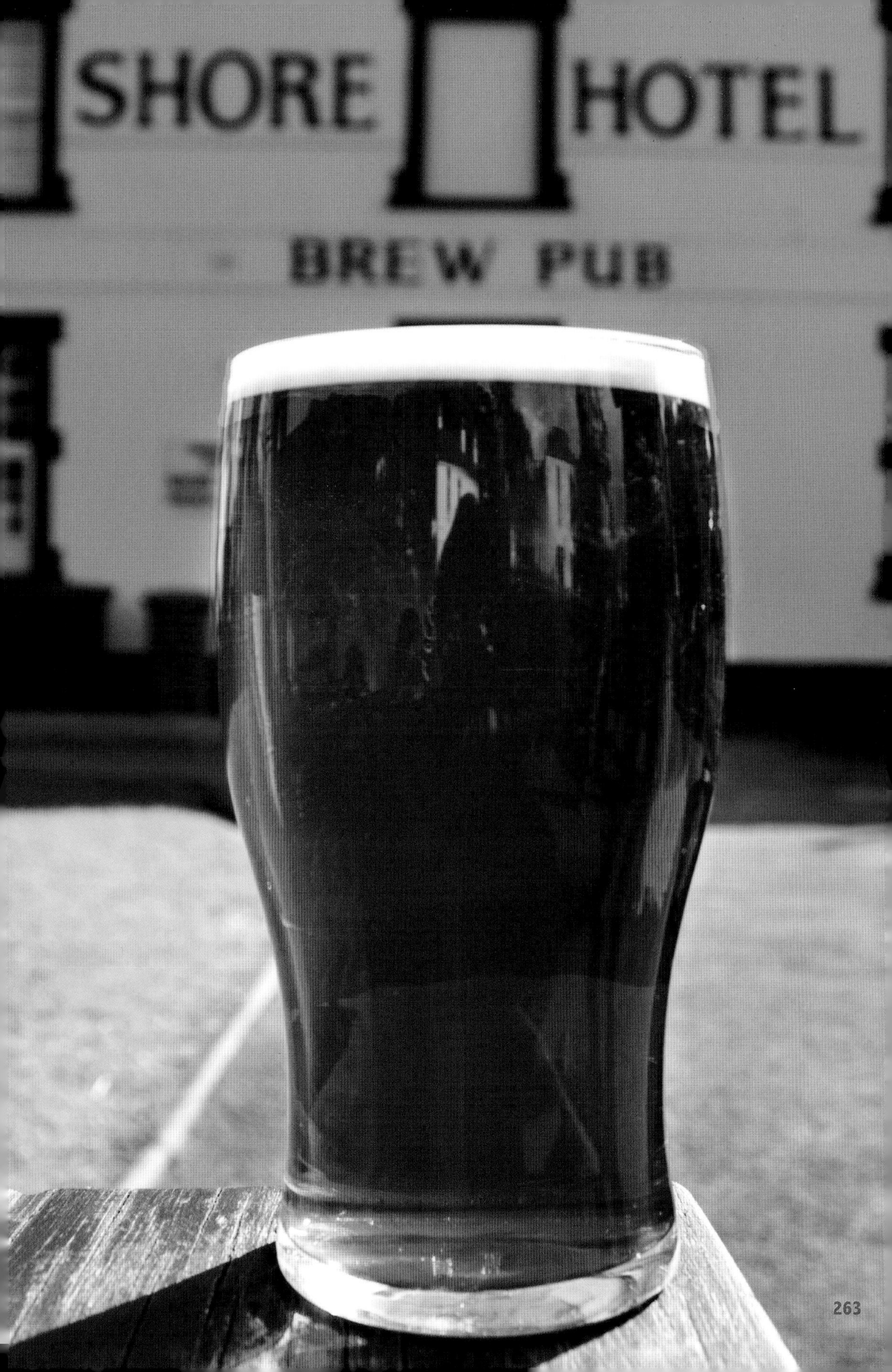
SHORE HOTEL
BREW PUB

APPLE ORPHANAGE

Apple Orphanage Co Ltd, The Lynague, German, Isle of Man IM5 2AQ
01624 439445 / 01624 315679
www.appleorphanage.com

Apple Orphanage Co Ltd is the fruit of Will Fauld's and Charlotte Traynor's labours. In 2009 we set out to make quality, handcrafted and truly Manx beverages using locally-grown, Manx ingredients. Specifically to make the most of what was already growing here on the Isle of Man.

So we came up with our Fruit Exchange. The idea is pretty simple: we press your surplus, home-grown crops and in return give you a fair share of the drinks that we make from them. We'd like everyone with an apple tree (or rhubarb plant etc.) to be able to enjoy delicious, freshly-pressed apple juice (or fruit pressé)… and for free!

We're passionate about keeping things natural and free from chemicals – we've realised you can make something taste great, we think better, without them and who wants to drink chemicals? So no concentrates, artificial flavourings or preservatives are used; just real, natural ingredients and fresh fruit harvested only a few miles away.

We produce a range of both soft and alcoholic drinks using Manx-grown apples, rhubarb, gooseberries and other fruits/vegetables adopted through our Fruit Exchange. We are always keen to experiment with new recipes that utilise any unused, wasted or forgotten fruit. Our range of drinks is limited only by our imagination and the fruits you bring us!

Minimising waste is something we strive to do throughout the business and our processes. All our bottles are heavy glass, which we recycle and reuse. Even the apple pulp we are left with after pressing is not wasted, but fed to our pigs who enjoy the apple season as much as we do!

Our Manx Apple juice is pure, unadulterated, pressed apples harvested via the Fruit Exchange. We press select apple cultivars to make a vast range of single-variety juices; from sweet to tangy, nutty to floral. There's a vast spectrum of flavours to enjoy and all without using any sugar or preservatives!

Our Manx Fruit Pressés are a little different – we experiment with traditional childhood favourites and locally-grown produce to create revolutionary, natural soft drinks with a fruity Manx twist!

Our original Manx Rhubarb Pressé and Manx Gooseberry Lemonade are particular favourites and seasonal pressés include: Cherry, Manx Elderberry and Cinnamon; Redcurrant, Manx Elderflower and Rosehip; Manx Spiced Blackcurrant; Manx Pear and Ginger; Manx Grape; Manx Plum Sasparilla and Manx Ginny Fizz (a wild nettle cola!).

To make our Manx Fruit Pressés we combine freshly-pressed Manx fruit with the finest, local, Green Mann Spring water. The mineral rich waters of

Green Mann Spring in Ballabrooie near St John's have been renowned for centuries. Rain falling on the slopes of Slieau Whallian has filtered down to create subterranean streams that flow beneath Balabrooie's beautiful orchards where organic practices have been followed for decades. Spring waters arise from hundreds of feet below ground, making the purest, most natural waters known to Mann, which we are very proud to use in our Manx Fruit Pressés.

Our Real Manx Dry Cider (5.4% ABV) is made from 100% Manx apple juice and nothing else! Fermented using wild yeasts and slowly matured over 12–24 months. The result is a dry, light-bodied and vinous cider with a crisp apple finish. Beautifully aromatic with a rich, deep apple bouquet.

Our Elderflower Keshal (3.5% ABV) is based on an old family recipe, which we've refined over the years. Made with Manx elderflowers our Keshal (Manx Gaelic for bubble/fizz) is a wonderfully fragrant, medium dry, naturally sparkling wine with a clean citrus finish.

We have relished the challenge of using unused, Manx fruit to create our drinks and look forward to creating new beverages using more fantastic local produce. We know buying local is not only healthy but important for our Island's future; we are thrilled to be developing relationships with local farmers who we are working with to re-appropriate small, underutilised pockets of land to grow more fruits and vegetables for us to press so we can keep making delicious, natural drinks out of the freshest, Manx-grown ingredients.

Join the fruit revolution!

THE HOODED RAM BREWING COMPANY

The Hooded Ram Brewing Company, Hills Meadow, Douglas, Isle of Man IM1 5EA
01624 612464
www.hoodedram.com

The Hooded Ram Brewing Company is the Island's newest microbrewery having only started brewing in September 2013. We are already award-winning, having received CAMRA Isle of Man Beer of the Festival 2015, 1st and 2nd place for Black Pearl Oyster Stout 5.2% and Little King Louis IPA 6.0% respectively, and previously 2014 1st place with Little King Louis IPA 6.0%.

The Brewery Bar is open on the first Friday of each month from 5–11 p.m. for Beer and Pie with no reservation necessary. Tours are offered on the second and third Fridays from 6.30 p.m. by arrangement.

Our beers are now widely available throughout the Island, with cask ales stocked in over 20 pubs and bottles available throughout many of the Island's hotels and restaurants.

Continuously available beers include:

Little King Louis IPA 6% – strong citrus notes, balanced malt and good bitterness are provided by:

MALT: Pale Ale, Lager, Wheat; HOPS: Bobek, Cascade, Amarillo

Amber Ram Best Bitter 4.3% – a well-balanced Best Bitter with enough hop and malt to keep those taste buds wanting more whilst balancing bitterness.

MALT : Pale Ale, Caramalt, Crystal, Wheat; HOPS: Pilgrim, Bramling Cross, Cascade

Jack The Ram Stout 4.7% – a classic stout with a good chocolate malt mouth feel, low hop aroma and balanced finish.

MALT : Pale Ale, Amber, Red Crystal, Chocolate; HOPS: Goldings, Fuggles

Robert decided to start brewing after becoming involved in the local CAMRA branch in 2010. Working in finance, and having no previous involvement in brewing, he booked himself onto a brewing course and resigned from his job whilst his wife, Shelly, was expecting their first child, Louis. Not quite a fully-fledged Manxman, Robert moved to the Isle of Man when he was four and was educated on the Island. Robert hopes the brewery will become the Island's small American style brewery producing a range of beers which aren't often available on the Island.

The brewery shop, located in Hills Meadow, is open Monday to Friday 9.00 a.m. to 5.00 p.m. and Saturday 10.00 a.m. to 2.00 p.m. Tours can be arranged by emailing info@hoodedram.com or calling the brewery on 01624 612464.

The **Hooded Ram Brewery Pub at Clinch's** opened in Summer 2016, for further information visit Facebook: https://www.facebook.com/Andy-The-Hooded-Ram-Brewery-at-Clinchs

CHAPTER 6
THE ISLAND'S LARDER OF FOOD

BAKERY & FLOUR

ABFAB CAKES

Contact: Anne Dorling
Available: Please contact me direct to place your order
T: 01624 627878 / 07624 404963
E: abfabcakes@manx.net Facebook: abfabcakesiom

ALLISON RATCLIFFE – MANXCAKEMAKER.COM

Contact: Allison Ratcliffe
Available: Available to order online, via Facebook or by
telephone
T: 07624 456123 E: allison@manxcakemaker.com
W: www.manxcakemaker.com

BERRIES LUXURY PUDDING MAKERS AND CONFECTIONERS

Contact: Karl or Natalie
Address: Aaron House, The Promenade, Port St Mary, Isle of
Man IM9 5DE
Available: Order online or by telephone between 9am and
6pm, Monday to Friday.
T: 01624 838384
E: info@berries.co.im W: www.berries.co.im

BISCUIT BARREL BAKERY

Contact: Lynn Owens
Available: Available at the farmers' markets at St Johns and
Ramsey
T: 01624 803246 / 07624 451115
E: lynn_owens@manx.net

BROWN COW BAKERY

Contact: Maggie or Chris Farmer
Available: Call or email your order direct.
T: 07624 439443 / 07624 401190
E: browncowbakery@manx.net

THE BUSY GLUTEN FREE KITCHEN

Contact: Simone Meadowcroft
Address: 31 Parliament Street, Ramsey IM8 1AT
Open: Tuesday to Saturday, 10am to 2pm, but check on
Facebook for updates
T: 07624 454152
E: thebusyglutenfreekitchen@manx.net
Facebook: The Busy Gluten Free Kitchen

THE DONUT FACTORY LTD

Contact: Steven Barrett, Joanne Callow
Address: 1 Bourne Place, Ramsey IM8 1JW
Open: Monday to Saturday, 10am to 6pm; Sunday, 11am to 4pm
T: 01624 819534
E: enquiries@donutfactory.co.im W: www.donutfactory.co.im

LAXEY GLEN MILLS LTD

Contact: Sandra Donnelly
Address: Laxey Glen Mills, Laxey
Open: Available at Laxey Glen Mills and at retail food stores
around the Island.
T: 01624 861202
E: customerservices@laxeyglenmills.com
W: www.laxeyglenmills.com

MANX PIES TOGO (2014) LTD

Contact: Adrian Darby or Rachel Cook
Address: 1C Manning House, Lord Street, Douglas, IM1 2BE
Open: Monday to Friday, 6.30am to 4pm
T: 01624 623507 / 07624 472965
E: info@manxpies-togo.com W: www.manxpies-togo.com

MUFFINS BAKERY

Contact: Anthony Morgan
Address: 21, Michael Street, Peel
Open: Monday to Saturday, 9am to 4.30pm
T: 01624 843194

RAMSEY BAKERY LTD

Contact: Sales team
Address: Ramsey Bakery, Station Road, Ramsey
Available: All Island delivery six days a week.
T: 01624 813604
E: jim@ramseybakery.com W: www.ramseybakery.com

SUZIE'S HOME BAKING

Contact: Suzie Holmes
Available: Come and see me at the farmers' markets at St Johns
and Ramsey. Orders by telephone most welcome.
T: 07624 350626 E: holme.susan@yahoo.com

TAYLOR MADE CAKES

Contact: Elaine Taylor
Address: n/a
Available: Please contact me direct to discuss your
requirements.
T: 07624 480739 E: elaine@taylormadecakes.co.im
Facebook: taylormadecakesiom

TIFFIN TEA ROOM CELEBRATION CAKES

Contact: Christine Lawrence
Available: Contact us to place your order.
T: 07624 481559
E: floralgateau@manx.net
Facebook floralgateau celebration and wedding cakes

DAIRY

AALIN DAIRY

Contact: Carl Huxham
Address: Cronk Aalin Farm, Sulby
Available: please contact me to place orders
T: 01724 469708 E: chuxham@hotmail.com
Facebook: Aalindairy

COOIL BROTHERS

Contact: Juan Hargreaves
Address: The Views Dairy Farm, Bradda Road, Port Erin
Open: Monday to Saturday, 6am to 7pm
T: 07624 420591 / 01624 836154
E: theviewscottage@manx.net or farmerj@manx.net

ISLE OF MAN CREAMERY

Contact: Customer Services
Address: Ballafletcher Farm Road, Tromode, Douglas
Open: Monday to Saturday, 9am to 5.30pm. Milk, cheese and cream are available from shops throughout the Island and can also be delivered direct to your doorstep.
T: 01624 632000
E: customerservices@isleofmancreamery.com
W: www.isleofmancreamery.com

DRINKS

Beers are brewed in the Isle of Man in accordance with the Isle of Man Pure Beer Act 1874 – which means that, unless approved by Tynwald, nothing can be used to substitute for malt, sugar or hops but other ingredients are added to create new brews.

BIFROST VODKA

Contact: Linda Keddie
Address: Kella Distillers Ltd, Kella Mill, Sulby IM7 2HH
Available: Available on the Island or from bifrostvodka.im
T: 01624 897777
E: info@bifrostvodka.im
W: www.bifrostvodka.im

GREEN MANN SPRING LTD

Contact: Shane Martin
Address: Ballabrooie, Patrick Road, St Johns
Open: Monday to Saturday, 8am to 5pm
T: 07624 321333 E: sales@greenmannspring.com
W: www.greenmannspring.com

MANX CIDER CO

Contact: Benn Quirk
Address: 12 Stanley Road, Peel
Available: Enjoy at selected pubs around the Island. Delivery service available.
T: 01624 843636 / 07624 380412
E: manxcider@hotmail.com   W: www.manxcider.co

MANX PACK LTD

Contact: Paul Wagstaff
Address: Unit 4, Balderton Court, Balthane Industrial Estate, Ballasalla
Available: Available from Shoprite stores and by appointment at Balthane.
T: 01624 824004
E: manx-pack@manx.net   W: www.manxteaandcoffee.com

ROOTS BEVERAGE COMPANY

Contact: Jamie Blair
Available: Stocked at Noa Bakehouse, 14North, Little Fish Café, Bath & Bottle, Thirsty Pigeon, Rileys Garden Centre, Mother T's, Patchwork Café, Green's Tea Rooms, Groudle Cottages, The Alpine, Freshly Squeezed and the Tea Junction
T: 07624 200015
E: Jamie@rootsbevco.im   Facebook: Roots Beverage Company

EGGS

BALLANORMAN COLOURED EGGS

Contact: Clare Lewis
Address: Ballanorman, Ballacrye Road, Ballaugh
Available: Please contact Clare prior to calling for eggs to check availability.
T: 07624 207555 E: clarelewis@manx.net
W: www.isleofmangoats.im

CLOSE LEECE FARM FREE-RANGE EGGS

Contact: Tracey Ridgway
Address: Close Leece Farm, Patrick Road, St John
Available: Available directly from the farm gate and selected retailers. Our eggs are also supplied directly to some of the best restaurants on the Island.
T: 07624 376343 E: tracey@ridgway.com

FARAGHERS MANX FREE-RANGE EGGS

Contact: Jackie Faragher
Address: Ballaseyre, Andreas
Open: Farm gate sales all day
T: 07624 458959 E: thefarm@manx.net

FINANN'S MANX FREE-RANGE EGGS

Contact: Ann Caine or Adrian Kinrade
Address: Shenvalla Farm, Glen Maye Road, Patrick
Open: daily
T: 07624 454037 / 07624 493616
E: annhorne@live.co.uk

GELLINGS FREE RANGE EGGS LTD

Contact: Mark Baines or Tracey Gelling
Address: Barroose Lane, Baldrine
Open: Monday to Saturday, 7.30am to 7.00pm
T: 07624 411530 / 07624 426363
E: gellingsfarm@hotmail.co.uk

PET POULTRY

Contact: Ruth Dermott
Address: Balladronnan Smallholding, Bollyn Road, Ballaugh IM7 5AY
Open: Please see our website for opening hours as they vary through the seasons
T: 07624 260555
E: petpoultry@gmail.com   W: www.petpoultry.im

SCOTTS OF GLEN MONA

Contact: Simon Scott
Address: Glen Mona House, Glen Mona, Maughold
Open: whenever you see our roadside 'Open' sign
T: 07624 435779 E: simonalistairscott@yahoo.co.uk

STAARVEY FARM ORGANIC EGGS

Contact: Stephen and Jenny Devereau
Address: Staarvey Farm, Staarvey Road, Peel, IM5 2AJ
Available: Available from Harrison and Garrett, Lee Mayers
Butchers, St John's Post Office, Tesco, Robinson's and Shoprite,
Douglas Farmers Markets and at the agricultural shows
T: 07624 463822 E: staarveyfarm@manx.net

FARM SHOPS, FARMERS' MARKETS, VEGETABLES AND NURSERIES

ALEXANDER NURSERIES

Contact: Tom Long
Address: Alexander Drive, Douglas
Open: Saturday 9am to 5.30pm
T: 01624 675829 E: alexandernurseries@manx.net

ALLANSON'S MANX PRODUCE

Contact: Stuart Allanson
Address: Rhendhoo Farm, Rhendhoo Road (C3), Jurby
Open: Monday to Friday, 9am to 5pm; Saturday, 9am to 1pm
(closed Bank Holidays)
T: 01624 880766 E: allansons@manx.net

BALLALEECE FARM SHOP

Contact: Margaret Kennaugh
Address: Ballaleece Farm, Peel Road, St Johns
Open: Friday to Saturday, 10.30am to 3pm
T: 01624 803269
E: johnkennaugh@hotmail.co.uk

BALLANELSON NURSERIES

Contact: Gill Kneale
Address: Ballanelson, Jurby East
Open: Monday to Sunday; 9am to 4pm
T: 07624 438588 / 07624 415900
E: gillkneale@yahoo.co.uk
Facebook: Ballanelson Nurseries

BALLAQUINNEY FARM

Contact: Maurice and Kevin Coole
Address: Ballaquinney Farm, Ballabeg, Ronague Road,
Castletown IM9 4HG
Available: Please contact us direct to place orders.
T: 01624 824125
E: coole@manx.net Facebook: Kevin Coole

BRY RAD'S FRESH VEG SHED

Contact: Bryan Radcliffe
Address: Farmers Combine, Quay Side, Ramsey or Rye Hill
Farm, St Judes, Andreas
Open: Shop at Famers Combine Saturday 9am to 4pm; farm
stall is open daily – honesty box provided.
T: 01624 880422 / 07624 458962
E: bryrad@manx.net
Facebook: Bry Rad's Fresh Veg Shed

CLEATOR'S FARM SHOP

Contact: Viv and Andrew Cleator
Address: Ballamenagh Beg, Sandygate IM7 3AG
Open: Monday to Sunday, 8am to 8pm
T: 07624 431585 / 07624 456957
E: cleator1952@live.co.uk
Facebook: Cleator's Farm Shop Sandygate

THE FARM SHOP – PICK YOUR OWN

Contact: Brian Moore
Address: Bibaloe Beg Road, Whitebridge Hill, Onchan
Open: June and July, Monday to Friday, 10am to 8pm; Saturday
to Sunday, 10am to 6pm; December, daily 10am to 6pm
T: 07624 495674
E: pyo@manx.net Facebook: Manx Strawberry Watch

THE FARMER'S DEN SHOP

Contact: Sheila Gawne
Address: Pooil Vaaish Farm, Castletown, IM9 4PH
Open: Open daily 9am to 5.30pm (winter), 9am to late
(summer). Also at farmers' markets around the Island.
T: 01624 822992 / 07624 454549
E: sbygroves@manx.net
Facebook: farmersdeniom

GARLIC MANN IOM

Contact: Alan Shimmin
Available: Please contact me to enjoy the health benefits of
this limited supply.
T: 07624 427066
E: garlicmanniom@manx.net Facebook: Garlicmanniom

GREENFIELD GARDEN CENTRE

Contact: Pascale Despringre
Address: Glencrutchery Road, Douglas
Open: Monday to Friday, 9am to 3.30pm; Saturday, 10am to
3.30pm in May, June and July
T: 01624 670849 E: Pascale.despringre@gov.im

MAGHER GRIANAGH FARM SHOP

Contact: Juan Howland
Address: Magher Grianagh Farm Shop, St Judes Road, Sulby
Open: 7 days a week
T: 07624 491941 E: juanhowland@manx.net

THE PLANT POT

Contact: Peter Skears
Address: 1 and 2 Plantation Cottages, Truggan Road, Port St
Mary IM9 5AX. The Plant Pot is just past the farm on the left.
Open: Tuesday to Sunday, 10am to 4pm
T: 07624 483117 / 01624 833117
E: peterskears@manx.net

PURELY PLANTS PRODUCE

Contact: Dot Price
Address: Ballacannell, The Dhoor, Lezayre IM7 43D
Open: Orders by telephone welcomed.
T: 01624 813358 / 07624 470507
E: dotprice@manx.net Facebook: Purely Plants Produce

STAARVEY FARM

For contact details see Page 270

We have been growing organically certified herbs and vegetable plants since 2006. We now produce organically certified mixed salad leaves, micro salad, freshly cut herbs and a selection of vegetables for local restaurants. Now available in retail packs in Robinson's and Shoprite.

ICE CREAM

DAVISON'S MANX DAIRY ICES

Contact: Ian or Greig Davison
Address: Davison's, The Factory, Mill Road, Peel
Shops: 3 Castle Court, The Promenade, Peel and The Chocolate Box, Castle Street, Douglas
Open: Peel: 9am to 8pm; winter 9.30am to 5pm; Douglas: 10am to 5.00pm
T: 01624 844111
E: ian.davison@davisons.co.im or greig@davisons.co.im
W: www.davisons.co.im

MANX ICES LTD

Contact: Jim Kearns
Address: The Cregg Mill, Silverdale Glen, Ballasalla IM9 3DS
Open: Summer 1 April to 30 September, Monday to Sunday, 10am to 5pm; Winter 1 October – 31 March, Saturday and Sunday, 10am to 5pm
T: 07624 493107 / 01624 823474
E: jim@manxices.com W: www.manxices.com

JAMS, PRESERVES, SAUCES AND OILS

Note that jams and preserves are also available at Farm Shops and farmers' markets – see separate sections.

ELLERSLIE RAPESEED OIL

Contact: Pentti Christian
T: 07624 472717
E: pentti.christian@brassicafoods.com
W: www.brassicafoods.com

MEAT, POULTRY & GAME

ANDREAS MEAT CO

Contact: Emma Pickard
Available: Buy our products from Shoprite and Robinson's as well as Ellan Vannin garages, selected Spar shops and other convenience stores.
T: 07624 306116 / 01624 880327
E: andreasmeatco@manx.net

BALLAKARRAN MEAT COMPANY

Contact: Will & Janette Qualtrough
Available: Orders taken via our website, by telephone or Facebook: page
T: 07624 398000 E: enquiries@ballakarran.com
W: www.ballakarran.com

BALLARAGH FARM LTD

Contact: Sam Quilleash
Address: Ballaragh Farm, Thie Eirinagh, Ballaragh, Lonan
Available: Please telephone to order
T: 07624 474747 E: samquilleash@hotmail.com

BALLAVAIR GALLOWAY – TRADITIONAL BEEF

Contact: Alison Teare
Address: Ballavair Farm, Bride Rd, Bride, Isle of Man
T: 07624 450296
E: teare@manx.net Facebook: BallavairGalloway

CROWVILLE POULTRY

Contact: Mrs D Moore
Address: Crowville Farm, Maughold
Available: Please contact me direct to discuss your requirements
T: 07624 457300 / 07624 368989
E: d-jmoore@manx.net

GLENFABA TAMWORTHS – RARE BREED PORK

Contact: Tracey Ridgway and Fiona Anderson
Address: Close Leece or Knockaloe Beg Farm, Patrick
Available: Keep in touch with us through our Facebook: page, email or text to see the latest litters and when they will be ready.
T: 07624 475330 / 07624 376343
E: info@glenfabatamworths.com
W: www.glenfabatamworths.com

GOOD LIFE

Contact: Penny or Carl Jewison
Address: Good Life Farm, West Loughan, Jurby
Available: Please contact us direct to place an order.
T: 07624 494949
E: penny@goodlife.im
W: www.goodlifefarm.im

ISLE OF MAN GOATS

Contact: Clare Lewis and Mike Walker
Address: Ballanorman, Ballacrye Road, Ballaugh
Available: Saturday, 1pm to 6pm for sales of goat meat and at other times by appointment
T 07624 207555 / 07624 222850
E: clarelewis@manx.net W: www.isleofmangoats.im

ISLE OF MAN MEATS

Contact: Customer Services
Address: Ballafletcher Farm Road, Tromode
Available: Please telephone to order
T: 01624 674346
E: info@iommeats.com W: www.iommeats.com

LEELA'S KITCHEN

Contact: Kumar Menon
Available: Delivered Island-wide. Spices available from major retailers around the Island. Gift vouchers available.
T: 07624 240200
E: leelaskitchen@manx.net W: www.leelaskitchen.co.uk

MAL'S BUTCHERS LTD

Contact: Malcolm Conley
Address: 35 Station Road, Port Erin
Open: Monday to Friday, 8.30am to 5pm; Saturday 8am to 4pm; Thursday until 7pm
T: 01624 832116 E: mals@manx.net

MANNBILTONG

Contact: David Robinson
Available: Our products can be found at Robinson's at Prospect Terrace, Douglas and we sell online and at various farmers' markets around the Island.
T: 07624 469416
E: mannbiltong@aol.co W: www.mannbiltong.co.uk

MANX BILTONG & BOEREWORS

Contact: Marc Gale
Available: Please contact me direct to place orders; produce available for collection or delivery
T: 017624 474544 / 07624 416254
E: marcgale@hotmail.co.uk

MICHAEL'S IN THE MARKET

Contact: Michael McNulty
Address: Market Hall, Market Hill, Douglas
Open: Monday to Thursday, 10am to 5pm, Friday and Saturday 9am to 5pm
T: 01624 623364

OXWAGON BILTONG AND BOEREWORS

Contact: Barry Butler-Smith
Available: Available at Robinson's, Shoprite, Iceland and selected health and fitness gyms and bars.
T: 07624 228108 E: barroley@hotmail.com

RADCLIFFE BUTCHERS

Contact: Chris Lennon
Address: 6 Malew Street, Castletown
 Open: Monday to Friday, 8am to 5pm; Saturday 8am to 2pm.
Shop online at and get your order delivered to your door
T: 01624 822271
E: sales@radcliffebutchers.com W: www.radcliffebutchers.com

SCOTTS OF GLEN MONA

Contact: Simon Scott
Address: Glen Mona House, Glen Mona, Maughold
Open: whenever you see our roadside 'Open' sign
T: 07624 435779 E: simonalistairscott@yahoo.co.uk

TEARE'S BUTCHERS

Contact: Mark Matthews
Address: WE Teare Ltd, 50 Parliament Street, Ramsey
Open: Monday to Saturday, 7.30am to 5.30pm
T: 01624 812460

SEAFOOD

CB HORNE ISLE OF MAN SEAFOOD PROCESSORS

Contact: Barry Horne
Address: The Isle of Man Food Park, Mill Road, Peel IM5 1TA
Open: Monday to Friday, 8am to 5pm
T: 07624 496347
E: barryhorne@manx.net W: www.cbhorne.com

CUSHLIN SEAFOOD

Contact: Allan Kermode
Address: Southview, Main Road, Ballaugh
Available: Please contact me direct for local sales – available for collection or delivery
T: 01624 898177 / 07624 437944

E: valeriek.2009@gmail.com

DESMOND'S FISH SHOP

Contact: Paul Desmond
Address; 23 Parliament Street, Ramsey
Open: Friday 9am to 3pm
T: 07624 496362 E: desmond@manx.net
W: www.manxkippers.com

DEVEREAU'S MANX KIPPERS

Contact: Tina and Barry Canipa
Address: 33, Castle Street, Douglas and Mill Road, Peel
Open: Monday 8am to 1pm; Tuesday to Saturday, 8am to 5pm
T: Douglas shop 01624 673257 / Peel shop 01624 843160
E: enquiries@isleofmankippers.com
W: www.isleofmankippers.com

THE FISH HOUSE

Contact: Patrick Croft
Address: Station Road, Promenade, Port St Mary IM9 5BF
Open: Monday to Thursday, 8am to 6pm; Friday, 8am to 6pm; Saturday, 8am to 4pm; Sunday, 9am to 2pm
T: 01624 833113 / 07624 204564
E: thefish-house@outlook.com W: www.thefish-house.co.uk

ISLE OF MAN SEAFOODS PRODUCTS LTD

Contact: Main Office
Address: Isle of Man Food Park, Mill Road, Peel
Open: Monday to Friday, 9am to 5pm
T: 01624 843739
E: info@isleofmanseafoods.com
W: www.isleofmanseafood.com

KALLOW POINT SEAFOODS

Contact: Aalish Maddrell or Christian Clugson
Available: Contact us direct for local sales
T: Aalish 07624 203133 / Christian 97624 483217
E: aalishm@yahoo.com

MANX FISH, PICKLES AND PATÉ

Contact: Antony Barrow
Address: 3 Athol Place, Peel and at the Swing Bridge, Peel
Open: Athol Place: Daily 9am to 7pm; Swing Bridge: Daily 10am to 7pm
T: 07624 477837

MOORE'S TRADITIONAL CURERS

Contact: Paul Desmond
Address: Mill Road, Peel
Available: Monday to Saturday, 9am to 5pm
T: 07624 496362

E: Desmonds@manx.net W: www.manxkipper.com